THE ORIGINS OF MONSTERS

The Rostovtzeff lectures are named for Michael I. Rostovzteff, a Russian ancient historian who came to the United States after the Russian Revolution and taught at the University of Wisconsin and then for many years at Yale University as Sterling Professor of Ancient History. Rostovtzeff's prodigious energies and expansive interests led him to write on an almost unimaginable range of subjects. The Institute for the Study of the Ancient World Rostovtzeff lecture series presents scholarship embodying its aspirations to foster work that crosses disciplinary, geographical, and chronological lines.

THE ORIGINS OF MONSTERS

Image and Cognition in the First Age
of Mechanical Reproduction

DAVID WENGROW

THIS WORK IS PUBLISHED IN ASSOCIATION WITH THE INSTITUTE FOR THE STUDY
OF THE ANCIENT WORLD AT NEW YORK UNIVERSITY.

PRINCETON UNIVERSITY PRESS
PRINCETON AND OXFORD

Published by Princeton University Press, 41 William Street,
Princeton, New Jersey 08540

In the United Kingdom: Princeton University Press, 6 Oxford Street,
Woodstock, Oxfordshire OX20 1TW

press.princeton.edu

Library of Congress Cataloging-in-Publication Data

Wengrow, D.
The origins of monsters : image and cognition in the first age of
mechanical reproduction / David Wengrow.
p. cm. — (The Rostovtzeff lectures)

Summary: "It has often been claimed that "monsters"—supernatural creatures with bodies composed from multiple species—play a significant part in
the thought and imagery of all people from all times. The Origins of Monsters advances an alternative view. Composite figurations are intriguingly
rare and isolated in the art of the prehistoric era. Instead it was with the rise
of cities, elites, and cosmopolitan trade networks that "monsters" became
widespread features of visual production in the ancient world. Showing
how these fantastic images originated and how they were transmitted, David
Wengrow identifies patterns in the records of human image-making and embarks on a search for connections between mind and culture. Wengrow asks:
Can cognitive science explain the potency of such images? Does evolutionary psychology hold a key to understanding the transmission of symbols?
How is our making and perception of images influenced by institutions and
technologies? Wengrow considers the work of art in the first age of mechanical reproduction, which he locates in the Middle East, where urban life
began. Comparing the development and spread of fantastic imagery across
a range of prehistoric and ancient societies, including Mesopotamia, Egypt,
Greece, and China, he explores how the visual imagination has been shaped
by a complex mixture of historical and universal factors. Examining the reasons behind the dissemination of monstrous imagery in ancient states and
empires, The Origins of Monsters sheds light on the relationship between
culture and cognition"— Provided by publisher.

Includes bibliographical references and index.
ISBN 978-0-691-15904-1 (hardcover)
1. Art, Prehistoric. 2. Art, Ancient. 3. Archaeology and art. 4. Animals,
Mythical, in art. 5. Cognition and culture. 6. Rostovtzeff,
Michael Ivanovitch, 1870–1952. I. Title.
N5310.W46 2013   704.9'4709—dc23
2013018192

British Library Cataloging-in-Publication Data is available

This book has been composed in Baskerville 10 Pro

Printed on acid-free paper. ∞

Printed in the United States of America

1 3 5 7 9 10 8 6 4 2

FOR JACK, MASTER OF TRANSFORMATION,

AND FOR CATHY URWIN (1949–2012), IN MEMORY

In the very first year there appeared from the Red Sea (the Persian Gulf) in an area bordering on Babylonia a frightening monster, named Oannes. . . . It had the whole body of a fish, but underneath and attached to the head of the fish there was another head, human, and joined to the tail of the fish, feet, like those of a man, and it had a human voice. Its form has been preserved in sculpture to this day. Berossos says that this monster spent its days with men, never eating anything, but teaching men the skills necessary for writing and for doing mathematics and for all sorts of knowledge: how to build cities, found temples, and make laws. It taught men how to determine borders and divide land, and also how to plant seeds and then to harvest their fruits and vegetables. In short, it taught men all those things conducive to a settled and civilized life. Since that time nothing further has been discovered.

—Berossos, *History of Babylonia*, Book 1
(after Verbrugghe and Wickersham 2001: 44)

Paleolithic art offers very few examples of what might be construed as flights of the imagination. Its monsters can be counted on the fingers of one hand.

—André Leroi-Gourhan, *Gesture and Speech*, 1993 [1964]: 393

CONTENTS

ILLUSTRATIONS

ACKNOWLEDGMENTS

∽⌣⌒

This book began life as the second series of M. I. Rostovtzeff Lectures, which I was honored to give at the Institute for the Study of the Ancient World, New York University, in the spring of 2011. My first thanks go to the faculty there, and in particular Roger Bagnall, for their confidence in my ability to address the academic mission of that institute, which pursues a connected vision of Old World cultures from prehistoric times to later antiquity. Both staff and students showed me enormous hospitality during my stay in New York, and responded with open minds to what were still, at that stage, a fairly raw set of ideas about the relationship between image, cognition, and institutional change. My second thanks go to the Institute of Archaeology at University College London, and especially Stephen Shennan, for granting me sabbatical leave to prepare those lectures and to develop them into the chapters that follow.

In doing so, I have been constantly reminded of the difficulties involved in approaching sources of evidence and bodies of theory outside my main areas of expertise, which lie in archaeology and anthropology (as opposed, for example, to cognitive science, ancient history, or art history, all of which play a role here). I hope that specialists working in other fields, especially those who gave so generously of their time and knowledge, will not find my treatment too cavalier, and that they will see this book primarily for what it is: an attempt to initiate dialogue between disciplinary approaches and area studies that are normally pursued in mutual isolation.

While none of the following can be held responsible for any of the arguments or evidence presented here, all will I hope accept my heartfelt thanks for their patience, interest, and much-needed advice: Bob Bagley, John Baines, Andy Bevan, Suzanne Blier, Maurice Bloch,

Philippe Descola, Lothar von Falkenhausen, Stephan Feuchtwang, Wang Haicheng, Bruce Kapferer, Susanne Küchler, Joseph Maran, John Mitchell, David Napier, Lukas Nickel, María Núñez, Asko Parpola, Dorit Peleg, Holly Pittman, Beate Pongratz-Leisten, Michael Puett, Stephen Quirke, Karen Radner, Jessica Rawson, Mike Rowlands, Erhard Schüttpelz, Stephen Shennan, Karen Sonik, Jeremy Tanner, Judith Weingarten, Irene Winter, and Norman Yoffee.

In preparing the book for publication, I have benefited from the experience and enthusiasm of Rob Tempio, Ali Parrington, and Ryan Mulligan at Princeton University Press, and from the generosity of those researchers who allowed me permission to use images from their work. I am grateful to all of them. My final thanks go as ever to my family and especially to Rinat Koren, who watched this project stumble from one false conclusion to another but never lost faith in my ability to complete it.

David Wengrow
London, 2013

THE ORIGINS OF MONSTERS

INTRODUCTION

The first age of mechanical reproduction belongs to Mesopotamia, and to the remarkable efflorescence of urban life that took place there some six thousand years ago. Its impact on visual culture, and on the history of design, has gone largely unnoticed. Walter Benjamin's famous (1936) essay on *The Work of Art in the Age of Mechanical Reproduction* looked no further back than the cast bronzes, terracottas, and coins of the ancient Greeks.[1] And when Henri Frankfort's compendious study of *Cylinder Seals* appeared three years later, it was as a *Documentary Essay on the Art and Religion of the Ancient Near East*,[2] rather than a treatise on the origins of print. Almost as quickly as it had emerged from the ground, the first age of mechanical reproduction disappeared from scholarly view. And the images it produced, in accordance with modern tastes and intellectual concerns, have found a new afterlife as singular works of art.

In this book, I reinstate the first age of mechanical reproduction as a context in which to discuss the relationship between image and cognition. Linking these various interests is the theme of "monsters,"[3] a term that I will shortly do away with and replace with "composites," which more accurately describes what I am interested in. That is, the early history of a particular kind of anatomical experiment, taking place in the visual domain. The essence of the experiment lay in isolating the limbs or other features of diverse species and recombining them to form images of beings that have no counterparts in the visible world. By a "history," I mean an analysis of how that experiment unfolded within a particular set of institutional and technological conditions, and what it contributed to the establishment and reproduction of those conditions.

Visual experiments of this sort are of course much older than urban life. As I will go on to discuss, they can occasionally be detected within the preserved record of prehistoric—Paleolithic and Neolithic—art. But their presence there is highly attenuated, almost to the point where one begins to suspect a pattern of deliberate avoidance. It is understandable that interpreters of prehistoric art, seeking clues to the origins of religious thought or symbolic expression, have placed great emphasis on the few surviving candidates. But this should not distract attention from the much stronger association between composite figures and the emergence of urban life, in the western part of the Old World, around six millennia ago.

Once established as subjects for regular depiction, images of composite beings often led remarkably cosmopolitan lives. They achieve distributions in the archaeological record that far outstrip those of other figural images, a pattern that continues into later periods of antiquity, beyond the scope of this book, the focus of which will be upon the Bronze Age (ca. 3000–1200 BC) with an eye to the Iron Age (ca. 1200–500 BC) as an axis of comparison. The distributions that I am referring to do not follow a random pattern: they are clearly associated with the expansion of political and commercial networks and, on a local scale, with the growth of urban settlements and the emergence of social elites—in other words, with the periods often labeled "proto," "archaic," or "formative"—because they precede the coalescence of cultural traditions into officially sanctioned canons or styles.

From the appearance of Mesopotamian composites in the art of protodynastic Egypt to the spread of "orientalizing" motifs in the Iron Age Mediterranean, the adoption of such images far beyond their source areas has long provided archaeologists with a sensitive tracer for the growth of commercial routes linking otherwise remote societies. Long-range image transfers of this kind are usually considered as isolated phenomena. I will suggest that, when viewed collectively, they provide evidence for a pattern of cultural transmission that unfolds with impressive consistency across chronological and cultural boundaries, inviting consideration in more general terms. In interpreting that pattern, I will be drawing upon recent approaches to the analysis of culture that are grounded in the study of cognition.

I will be particularly, though not exclusively, concerned with a body of theory called the "epidemiology of culture." Developed on the cusp of evolutionary anthropology and cognitive psychology, and most closely associated with the work of Dan Sperber and Pascal Boyer,[4] its goal is to explain the differential spread and durability of cultural representations in terms of evolved biases in human cognition. Such theories, as currently formulated, have been applied mainly to language-based aspects of culture. They offer no ready-made methodology for understanding the relationship between cognition and the transmission of a wider range of cultural practices, artifacts, or institutions; nor were they designed with a view to the analysis of visual images or archaeological data. My aim, in relating them to material of the latter kind, is not to "fit square pegs into round holes." It is rather to probe the boundaries of analytical fields that claim, in the last resort, to be addressing a common problem: the unified understanding of culture as a product of both history and cognition.

As Barbara Stafford observes, one of the greatest attractions of a rapprochement between cognitive and cultural studies is the promise of deeper insight into "the potency and longevity of certain types of representation."[5] The desire for such a rapprochement is increasingly felt in archaeological and anthropological research,[6] as well as in art history. Major cultural turning points such as the earliest appearance of pictorial art, the invention of farming, and the development of writing, mathematics, and metrical systems, are now often considered not only as technological transformations but also as transformations in modes of thought.[7] Bridging the disciplinary gap between cognitive psychology and archaeological reconstructions of the past is, however, a complex and risky affair. A brief example of the pitfalls will serve to further introduce the main theme and problematic of this book.

Cognitive psychologists in the 1990s proposed that our ability, as a species, to generate mental images of impossible beings (three-headed men, horses with wings, and so on) may have evolved in tandem with our capacity for complex social interaction. The hypothesis derived from controlled experimental studies in which children who exhibit behavioral deficits in social interaction and imaginative expression were asked to produce drawings of creatures that do not exist. By comparison with typically developing children, they performed poorly in this task.[8] The study, tentative in its conclusions, was subsequently incorporated into archaeological debates concerning the interpretation of prehistoric art. In light of its findings, it was proposed that the rendering in Upper Paleolithic rock art of composite figures—such as the famous "Sorcerer" of Les Trois Frères (shown later in figure 3.1b), whose body comprises both human and animal parts—may have reinforced the development among early hunter-gatherers of cognitive capacities for complex symbolic communication that would otherwise have remained latent.[9]

It may be surprising for some readers to learn that, despite established critiques (such as those mounted by the anthropologist A. Irving Hallowell in the mid-twentieth century),[10] behaviors observed in modern infants are still being used to frame hypotheses about the evolution of human cognition in prehistoric times. In this particular instance, it was subsequently demonstrated that, under modified experimental conditions, children with the same range of behavioral symptoms are, in fact, perfectly able to draw pictures of imaginary beings, including anatomical composites.[11] Experimental psychology is a fast-moving field, and evolutionary hypotheses based on an uncritical acceptance of its findings are inherently fragile.

But there are other methodological issues at play. Data for psychological experiments of the kind described often derive from controlled observations of how subjects make and perceive images.

It is commonly assumed, in the course of such experiments, that physical images provide faithful reflections of evolved, mental representations, projected mirror-like onto the material world. But the creation and perception of images is always mediated by other factors, of which cultural historians have long been aware. They include sensory-motor skills, developed in relation to particular tools and materials, and socially learned expectations about what can and cannot be seen in the world.[12] Cultural historians might then be inclined to ask how far the boundaries of visual imagination are set by nurture rather than nature, over historical rather than evolutionary timescales.

For instance, an Egyptologist noting the routine appearance of griffins among the (real) desert animals mentioned or depicted in ancient Egyptian sources has commented:

> We should recognize that our categorization of "real" and "imaginary" animals is far from being an objective criterion of universal applicability. An ancient Egyptian would have reckoned with the possibility of really encountering a griffin, especially if walking around in the area near the Red Sea coast, and there is even a demotic tale telling of a griffin that comes from the Red Sea and wreaks havoc among the Egyptian army.[13]

At least some evolutionary psychologists would want to qualify that statement. They would point out that openly stated beliefs in the reality of griffins or dragons—while perfectly valid within certain cultural contexts—are likely to be of a different cognitive order to beliefs in living species, including species that we may never encounter in reality. The reason they would give is that human minds possess a hard-wired mechanism for classifying and processing information about living kinds of plants and animals.[14] That mechanism evolved over many thousands of years through adaptation to ancestral environments in which things such as griffins and dragons did not exist. Cultural norms may suppress, exploit, or manipulate those innate neurological dispositions, but cannot override them entirely.

Theoretical and philosophical debates have so far done little to bridge the chasm between constructivist and biological understandings of human cognition. The current impasse and the increasing specialization of cognitive neuroscience have allowed many in the humanities and social sciences to beat a quiet retreat into apparently more familiar territory, even as the analytical ground on which they work is shifting beneath their feet. Anthropological understandings of cognition, as Susanne Küchler observes,[15] are similarly torn between extremes: the notion of autopoiesis through an "embodied mind," flexibly learning to cognize its surroundings through tactile encounters with a culture-laden world, and the opposing (but no less romantic) notion of a pristine and immutable hunter-gatherer brain, still fighting its primeval battles through recalcitrant cultural terrain, in a modern situation of its own mysterious making.

In an effort to break this deadlock, and to broaden the debate beyond the domain of language, both Küchler and Stafford have highlighted the role of physical objects as nonhuman bearers of thought-like processes, carrying "images that make shared learning possible."[16] The advent of artificial intelligence, they point out, has taken the notion of animated objects far beyond the realms of metaphor and theory, locating it at the center of current knowledge economies and communicative practice. Rather than taking this development to mark an unbridgeable rupture with the past, they ask how, in preelectronic and predigital worlds, images—and their media of transmission—may nevertheless have encapsulated forms of associative reasoning that do not simply encode what is already in the mind but also organize thought into patterns that are historically and culturally distinctive.[17]

Images of composite animals pose a series of interesting conceptual problems in this regard. Their transmission can be interpreted via two very different notions of modularity, one rooted in cognition and the other in technology. From the perspective of evolutionary psychology they can be viewed as "taxonomic aberrations,"[18] activating a dedicated neurological device (or "mental module") for the recognition of living kinds, but at the same time confounding its expectations by combining elements from different species or genera. This point is complex, and I will return to it in more detail. But composite bodies are also the products of another kind of modularity, which is concerned with the practical and conceptual division of the physical world (including the world of images) into standard and interchangeable subunits. Although their respective starting points are very different—one beginning inside the mind and the other outside the body—both concepts of modularity have implications for cultural transmission, and as I will try to show, the early history of the composite figure obliges us to address the relationship between them.

It was in fact an ancient historian, Mikhail Rostovtzeff, for whom these lectures in their original form were fortuitously named, who first pointed out an association between the earliest expansion of urban life and the spread of what he termed "fantastic creations formed by the amalgamation of favorite animals of the period with each other and sometimes with human beings."[19] My first chapter asks what led him almost a century ago to compare distributions of composites from China to Scandinavia, and to seek links between them. In the remainder of this book, I consider—from various perspectives—how the distribution of composite figures in the visual record offers fertile testing ground for an "epidemiological" approach to culture, and ultimately forces a revision of some of its central assumptions. In doing so, I offer a number of general observations about the relationship between image, cognition, and early state formation in the western Old World.

1

IMAGE AND ECONOMY IN
THE ANCIENT WORLD

THE BRONZE AGE OF MIKHAIL ROSTOVTZEFF

Mikhail Ivanovich Rostovtzeff (1870–1952) is remembered most often today for his seminal studies of Greco-Roman antiquity, and for his controversial—some might say untenable—view that the true architects of classical civilization were not those tied to the land, whether as peasant laborers or feudal aristocracy, but rather the middling professional classes of merchants, industrialists, and bankers whose social aspirations were most closely in tune with the civic values of an expanding urban society.[1] In reviewing Rostovtzeff's monumental work on the social and economic history of the Roman Empire, Glenn Bowersock notes that "he presupposed a capitalist society which itself presupposed the primacy of commerce and industry" as guiding influences upon the course of history.[2] Rostovtzeff therefore represents one side of an ongoing debate over the nature of economic life in the ancient world, and the extent to which the forms and functions of ancient economies can be understood through the lens of modern experience.[3]

Rostovtzeff's life and work has been the subject of several notable studies, written mostly by experts on the classical world.[4] This may explain a relative lack of attention to those features of his scholarship that an archaeologist, working on earlier periods, might find most intriguing. They relate less to his championing of the bourgeoisie than to the sheer scale—both spatial and chronological—on which he tried to pursue a complex argument about the relationship between economic forces and cultural change, and also to the variety of historical sources that he brought into account. For Rostovtzeff, the civilizing role of commerce and capital (as opposed to agrarian values and dynastic authority) was not to be reconstructed just on the basis of fiscal records and other textual sources. It could also be detected in the material culture of tribal, nonliterate societies, and most notably in the elaborate styles of imagery that they produced, circulated, and wove together with a consummate skill that still commands our admiration (figure 1.1).

Following on the heels of his (1922) *Iranians and Greeks in South Russia*, we find a series of lectures on *The Animal Style in South Russia and China*, delivered at Princeton and published in 1929. I will return to those lectures, and to the subject of China, in chapter 5. The former study laid foundations for an internal account of seminomadic civilization on the Russian steppe, relying mainly on archaeological discoveries, instead of the written accounts of Scythian and Sarmatian culture provided by Greek commentators. Rostovtzeff highlighted the prominence of cosmopolitan display items, procured from urban trading partners, in the tombs of the steppe kings. He took this as evidence that their wealth and power was grounded in access to commercial routes flanking the great patchwork of grasslands between the Danube and the Yellow River. The steppe acted as a kind of cultural cauldron in which otherwise unrelated elements of urban civilization were drawn together in novel combinations, and disseminated farther afield. This was most apparent in the intense fusion of visual styles and techniques to be found in nomadic art, echoes of which could be detected from the northern frontiers of China to Celtic Europe.[5]

Still more striking are Rostovtzeff's attempts to find traces of this commercial and cosmopolitan impulse amid the evidence of pre- and protohistoric societies.[6] This interest in the deep origins of Old World civilizations becomes more understandable in the context of Rostovtzeff's exile from his native Russia, at age forty-eight. It provided a way of suggesting that Bolshevik communism, far from

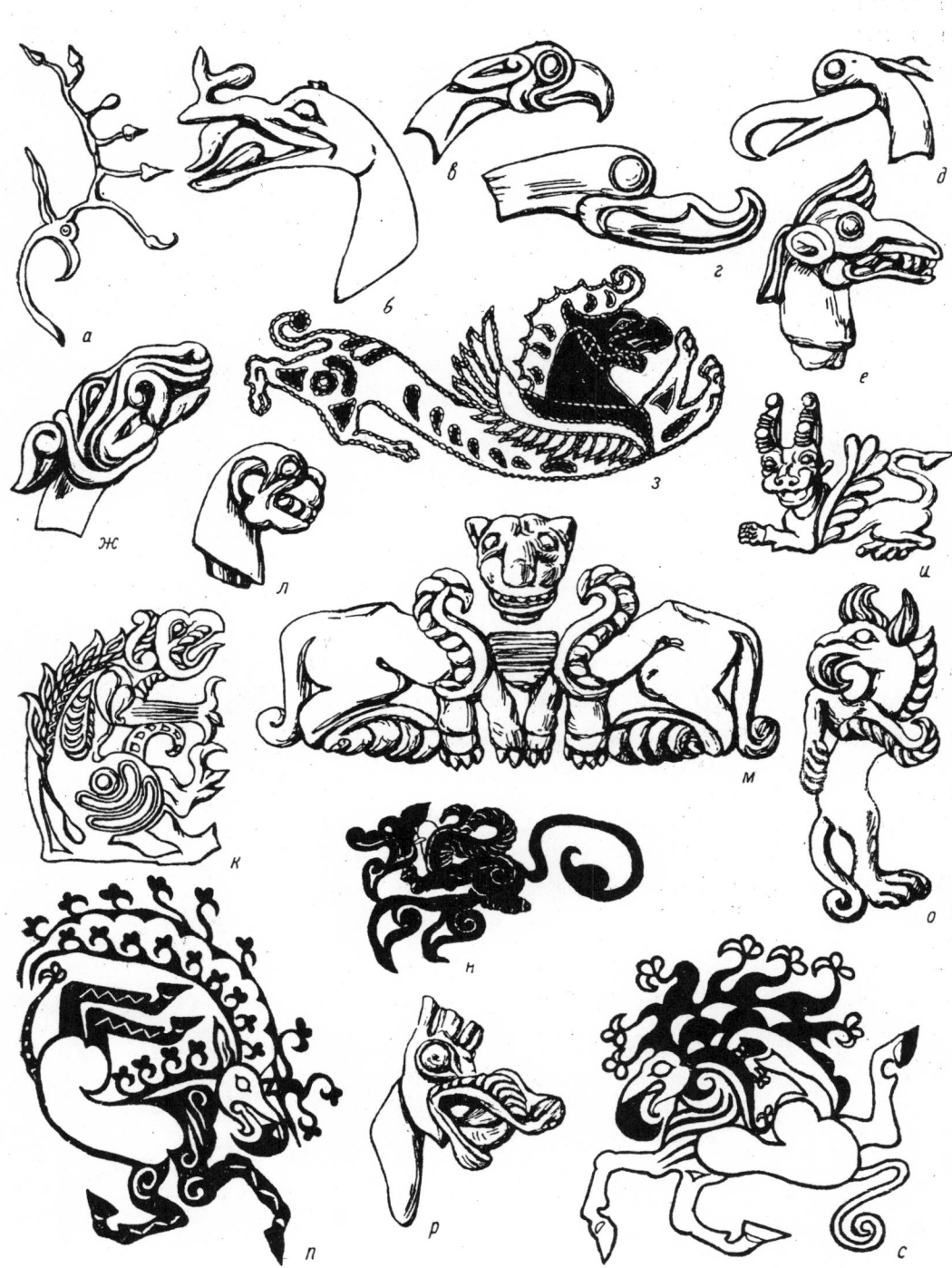

being the culmination of a long evolutionary process, was an anomalous departure from the values that had shaped Europe's development over the millennia.[7] Alongside studies of Greco-Roman economy and society, we find Rostovtzeff embroiled in debates over the chronological position and cultural affiliations of Bronze Age metal hoards, unearthed along the shores of the Caspian and Black Seas.[8] With remarkable perspicacity, he discerned relationships among the elite iconography of protodynastic Egypt, Mesopotamia, Elam, and the Caucasus, some of which I will be considering in the chapters that follow. And in *Iranians and Greeks*, we discover a cultural genealogy for the fantastic beasts of Scythian art, reaching back to the first Bronze Age states on the Tigris and Euphrates. The wider implications were fairly clear: feudalism had not emerged from the closed, command economies of Marx's "Asiatic mode of production," but from an interconnected world of remote antiquity, bound together by shared commercial interests.

It is, perhaps, worth trying to relate these prehistoric interests a little more closely to Rostovtzeff's better-known work on later periods of antiquity. *Caravan Cities*, published in 1932, was a more personal account of the classical remains at Petra, Jerash, Palmyra, and also Dura-Europos, on the Syrian Euphrates, where Rostovtzeff had excavated. Its opening chapter, tracing the Bronze Age origins of the caravan trade in the Near East, demonstrates an acute awareness of archaeological evidence as a window onto far-flung connections, linking the development of ancient societies. The first great alluvial civilizations of Sumer and Egypt, he noted, were dependent on remote highland sources for supplies of metal, ivory, rare woods, precious stones, spices, cosmetics, pearls, and "incense for

1.1. Images of fantastic creatures from the Pazyryk and Tuekta *kurgans*, South Russia, seventh to fourth century BC (after S. I. Rudenko. 1960. *Kul'tura naseleniia tsentral'nogo Altaia v Skifskoe vremia*. Moscow/Leningrad: Izd-vo Akademii nauk SSSR, fig. 148).

the delectation of gods and men." The archaeological distribution of luxury consumables, commercial instruments, and political symbols confirmed that "the oldest city-states of Sumer in Mesopotamia were linked to far distant lands by caravans: to Egypt in the west, to Asia Minor in the north, to Turkestan, Seistan, and India in the east and south-east."[9]

Archaeologists, such as V. Gordon Childe and Henri Frankfort, would later add substance to this historical sketch of a connected Bronze Age world, reaching from the Indus to the Mediterranean, bound together through commerce in rare and precious commodities.[10] The chapters that follow will explore that world in greater detail. First, however, there is more to say about Rostovtzeff's approach to images, and how it defines my own task.

CELEBRATING MONSTERS

By the early decades of the twentieth century, the study of prehistoric and ancient art in continental Europe had become strongly associated with questions of racial identity and national spirit. The influence of Alois Riegl (1858–1905), and his concept of *Kunstwollen*, was especially strong in Austria and Germany.[11] As Jas Elsner points out, the period in which Riegl's followers developed his new science of the visual arts was also that in which Mendelian genetics were first applied to questions of inheritance and variability among natural species. The common analytical factor, which Elsner also detects in Gestalt psychology, was faith in the idea that minute and critical study of form would eventually lay bare the workings of a grand totality.[12]

Applied to culture, this paradigm could only incorporate the mixing of local and foreign elements in somewhat ambivalent terms. Hence Riegl, writing of the famous Bronze Age cups from Vapheio near Sparta, could acknowledge a technological debt to Oriental craftsmanship, while insisting that the borrowings had been of a purely technical nature, serving only to augment a preexisting cultural milieu that remained steadfastly Greek, and hence European. Half a century before the decipherment of the Linear B script, which demonstrated the Bronze Age roots of Classical Greek language, he already felt able to write, on the basis of the golden cups and their relief decoration, that "the Mycenaean period heralds the people who would later invent philosophy and the natural sciences and who would create the notion that man is the measure of all things."[13]

Riegl did not live to see the publication of Fredrik Poulsen's (1912) study of orientalizing influences upon archaic Greek art. Poulsen's achievement was to lay out, with unprecedented clarity, a range of evidence for the movement of artistic techniques and motifs—including a variety of composite creatures—from the western fringes of the Neo-Assyrian Empire to the Aegean and central Mediterranean, in the centuries preceding the formation of the classical Greek canon (figure 1.2).[14] Perhaps it is wrong to speculate as to whether Riegl would have agreed with the view of some later historians, who interpreted orientalizing art as a kind of unpleasant inoculation, which Greek culture had to endure in order to realize its native genius. But at a time when social fears about a contemporary "Eastern Problem" ran high in Europe, there seemed an obvious significance to the infiltration of Greek art by "monstrous" forces at its point of gestation, and their subsequent "taming" within a native scheme of representation.[15]

It is against this background that we can begin to appreciate the distinctiveness of Rostovtzeff's approach to the interpretation of imagery, and his particular attraction to the imaginary creatures of nomadic art. He seems to have delighted in the unbounded character of these particular designs, following their transmission far and wide, across the boundaries of urban and pastoral, literate and nonliterate, societies. In addition to their innately hybrid character—as depictions of fantastic, composite species—the images whose distribution he so carefully traced are also the outcome of cultural admixtures and borrowings, fusing technical knowledge of diverse media and

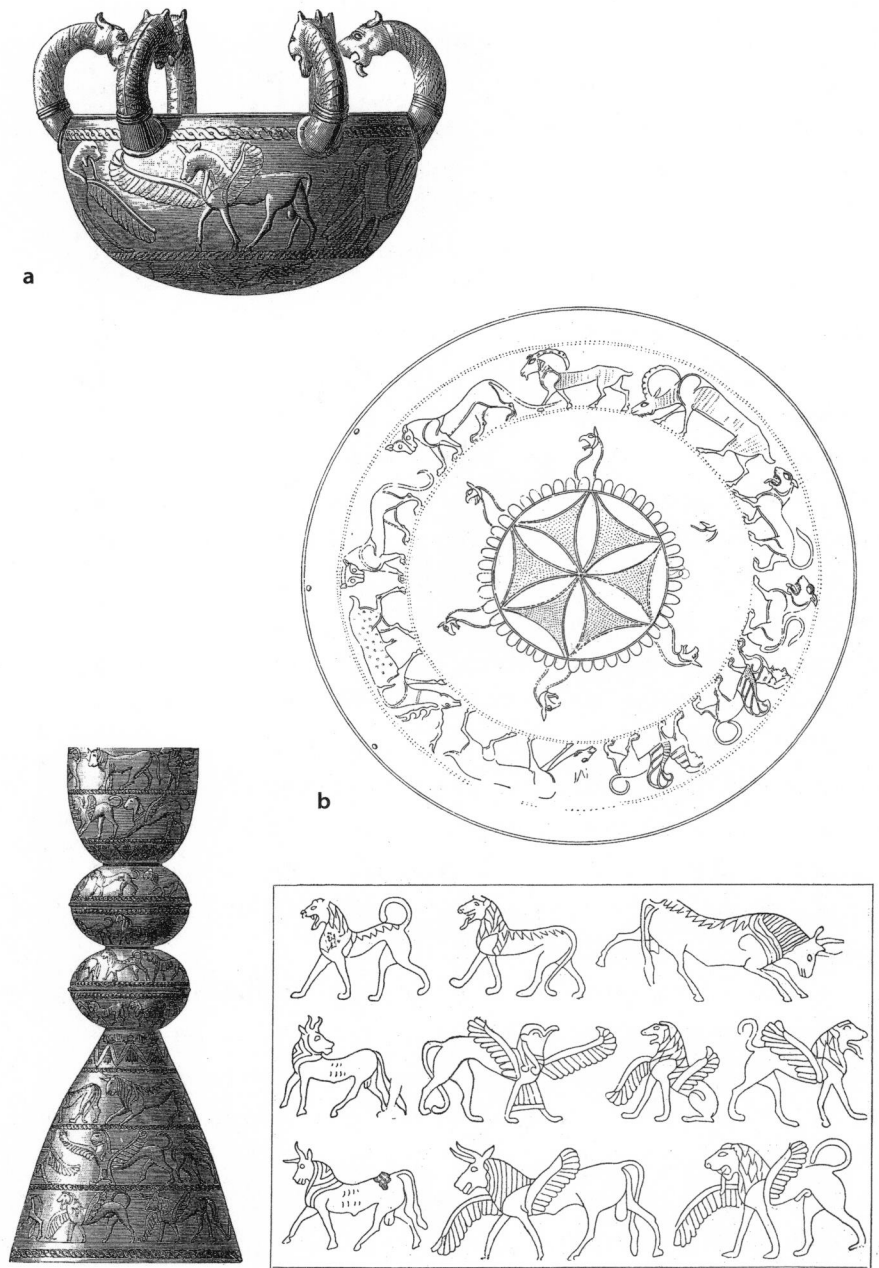

a

b

c

modes of representation from multiple societies. And yet, as he intimated, we typically find these depictions on the surfaces of artifacts that possessed strong local significance as ritual or magical objects, through the use of which each individual society forged its own special relationship to the gods.

It might be argued that these movements of monsters, seemingly promiscuous and endlessly adaptive, offered a kind of visual counterpart to Rostovtzeff's story of an ever-expanding Bronze Age civilization, evolving by virtue of its receptiveness to outside influence, and its ingenuity in weaving together the local and the foreign. As a template for the interpretation of social history, however, this attempt to project *Homo economicus* onto the world of images—if such it was—was scarcely less idealized than the myths of cultural autochthony that it sought to displace. Image and economy are connected in Rostovtzeff's work through their distributions in time and space, rather than by any causal or functional relationship. We search in vain for any attempt to account for the fact that, over a period of millennia, the nomadic elite of the Russian steppe not only commissioned and accumulated exotic wealth from an urban hinterland but also sacrificed it to the ground in spectacular burial rites, creating a monumental landscape of *kurgan* mounds that extended from the Altai to the Black Sea (ensuring, in the process, the physical preservation of objects and images that have largely disappeared from their areas of manufacture).

It is not difficult, with hindsight, to see why Rostovtzeff avoided such matters. In the 1920s and 1930s, they would have brought him into the uneasy company of the Frankfurt- and Vienna-based

1.2. (a, b) Sheet-bronze vessels and (c) stand with relief decoration, engraving, and repoussé, from Central Italy (a, c) and Rhodes (b), seventh century BC (after F. Poulsen. 1912. *Der Orient und die frühgriechische Kunst*. Leibzig: B. G. Teubner, figs. 86, 135–137).

Kulturkreislehre, or still worse perhaps, the hyper-diffusionist school of prehistory, which was busily tracing the movement of Egyptian cults and esoteric signs across the Atlantic, borne aloft on the slimmest of evidence.[16] Yet an unwillingness to consider functional, as opposed to merely distributional, relationships between the spread of representations and the expansion of commerce is equally evident in Rostovtzeff's reconstructions of later antiquity. Following his gaze around the ruins of Jerash, Petra, or Palymra, it is the ritual landscape of sacred springs and pathways, ornate rock-cut tombs, and stone temples adorned with cult statues that command our attention, but their links to the mundane world of the market, theater, public bath, and household remain unclear.[17]

What, then, has Rostovtzeff bequeathed to the study of preclassical antiquity that might be of lasting value? Different people will have different answers, but the legacy that interests me, and that I propose to develop, concerns the links he explored between large-scale distributions of images and the growth of commercial and political networks. It is understandable, given the fragmentary nature of his evidence, that Rostovtzeff should have contented himself with tracing the outlines of these relationships, leaving aside questions of causation. He did, however, propose one specific avenue of inquiry, which remains relatively unexplored, and which I will adopt as my own point of departure. It concerns the sporadic transmission, across cultural boundaries, of certain distinctive kinds of image.

FANTASTIC IMAGES AND THE GROWTH OF NETWORKS

In *Iranians and Greeks in South Russia,* Rostovtzeff drew attention to what he perceived as an important innovation in visual culture, tracing its source to the third millennium BC, and to ancient Sumer: the world's first literate and urban civilization, located on the southern plains of Mesopotamia. Today we would extend this search for origins back at least to the fourth, or perhaps the late fifth, millennium. The innovation was, as he put it, "the introduction into decorative and symbolic art of special symbolic and fantastic creations formed by the amalgamation of favourite animals of the period with each other and sometimes with human beings."[18]

Rostovtzeff never made fully clear what he viewed as the significance of this development. The following passage of his text leaves no doubt that, for him, the point was not going to be one about the symbolic workings of a collective unconscious. This he left to the analytical psychologists, and to their intellectual counterparts in art history. Instead it resided in the empirical distribution of particular images (and particular ways of crafting images) along certain pathways of cultural transmission, and the historical connections and responses generated by such spreads: "It was thus," he went on, "that the popular types of fantastic animals with a religious significance arose: the two types of griffin—with a horned lion's head, and with an eared eagle's head, both crested; the two types of dragon—with a snake's or a crocodile's head, horned or not; the well-known type of the sphinx. All these types spread far and wide, eastward, westward, and northward."[19]

In the last statement, Rostovtzeff has already departed from the art historical orthodoxy of his day, abandoning a strictly "orientalizing" framework of interpretation—focused upon the Greek world—for one that places equal emphasis on north- and eastward movements of culture.[20] At this critical point, however, his argument becomes enigmatic, increasing markedly in scope, but little in clarity:

> I cannot dwell upon this subject either. I must point out, however, that the Sumerian innovations exercised a powerful influence upon the entire ancient world. The influence can be observed everywhere, in Egypt, in Hittite Asia Minor, in Babylonia and Assyria, in the Aegean and Mycenaean world, in Cyprus and in Phoenicia, in Phrygia, Lydia, Cappadocia, Paphlagonia,

Lycia, in Etruria and in Sardinia, and finally in continental, island and colonial Greece.[21]

But Greece did not, in fact, mark the end of the monsters' trail. Rostovtzeff goes on to note that in Mesopotamia, the heartland of monsters, further mutations took place throughout the first millennium BC, producing new generations of fantastic beasts. As though spurred on by a sudden realization, he documents the transfer of this new bestiary into Iranian art, whence it flowed into the Scythian animal style, departing both northward "to the forests and swamps" of temperate Europe, and eastward, to the frontiers of China.[22] So, he thought, these fabulous creatures had found their way, through diverse routes of contact and transmission, onto the surfaces of funerary offerings presented to the gods of the Danube and the Yellow River, to be received with equal grace by both.

MATERIALS FOR AN EPIDEMIOLOGY OF CULTURE

Rostovtzeff's exploratory mapping of composite figures contains the seeds of a more focused study on the relationship between cognition and cultural transmission. After a century of archaeological and art historical research, the map, of course, will need to be heavily redrawn. To attempt this on a comprehensive scale would today require a volume, or perhaps a number of volumes, many times larger than this one. So I will focus, in the chapters that follow, on establishing where the main contours of the distribution lie: its zones of greatest and least intensity, how they shift around, and what other phenomena their movement might relate to. First, however, I will set out the justification for this remapping exercise, as well as a more precise definition of its subject matter, beginning with a discussion of composite animals as counterfactual images.

COUNTERINTUITIVE ELEMENTS IN THE TRANSMISSION OF CULTURE

Experimental studies show that the cognitive processing of animal forms is highly sensitized to part-whole relations, such that a total presence may be inferred from quite limited visual cues.[1] Pictures of animals—even when jumbled, distorted, or incomplete—may therefore activate neural pathways attuned to the recognition and differentiation of living kinds. Images that ostentatiously combine elements from different species—what Barbara Stafford calls "compressive compositions"—draw attention to these otherwise unconscious processing mechanisms, foregrounding the human mind's ability to compensate for absences in the visible world, and its capacity to conjure organic-seeming wholes out of "individualistic, competing, and fissionable parts."[2]

Such observations allow us to build bridges between the cognition of images and theories of cultural transmission. Here I will be particularly concerned with a school of evolutionary psychology called the "epidemiology of culture,"[3] which has so far focused mainly on the transmission of concepts through language. The analogy is not so much with the spread of diseases as with the analytical resolution at which epidemiologists address problems of distribution. A basic requirement of this approach, as with other neo-Darwinian approaches to cultural transmission,[4] is that the distribution of cultural facts should be studied at the level of "populations." What this means is that distributions should not be approached within predefined boundaries—whether those of the sedentary group, the nation-state, or as given by geographical circumstances—but at their fullest observable extent. Only then is it possible to assess their conditions of expansion, and to establish why some elements of culture are more able than others to spread and to become stable within larger fields of transmission.[5]

A second principle of the epidemiological approach is that these macro-distributions should be accounted for in terms of processes taking place at the micro-scale of human interaction.[6] It is here that cognitive capacities and constraints come into play. A significant body of research suggests that our everyday perception of the world is shaped by a modular pattern of cognition.[7] Mental modules are specialized neurological learning devices, attuned to the acquisition and processing of knowledge within particular domains of experience. Language acquisition, mathematical reasoning, and facial recognition are examples of such domains, which have received attention from developmental psychologists and neurobiologists.[8] Another is the capacity to interpret the behavior of others in terms of mental states like belief and desire (so-called theory of mind), a prerequisite for competence in social interaction.[9] It is hypothesized that this modular formatting of the mind-brain took place at an early stage in the evolution of our species, through interaction with environments very different from those we now inhabit. As part of our species-wide genetic inheritance, it has nevertheless continued to shape cultural transmission and innovation along certain pathways.

Modular reconstructions of human cognitive processes—and in particular the kind of "massive modularity" required by the epidemiology of culture—are not uncontroversial. The neurological basis of the approach therefore remains open to question and revision.[10] In probing the relationship between cognition and culture, it nevertheless seems preferable to work within the bounds of an established hypothesis, rather than with some more vague or implicit notion of "how the mind functions." Sperber and Hirschfeld propose that tangible artifacts, as well as spoken discourse, may stimulate specific mental modules, thus enhancing their chances of transmission:

> For instance, face recognition modules found in primates accept as input simple visual patterns that in a natural environment are almost exclusively produced by actual faces. In the human cultural environment, a great many artifacts are aimed at the face recognition module. They include portraits, caricatures, masks and made-up faces. The effectiveness of these cultural artifacts is in part explained by the fact that they rely on and exploit a natural disposition.[11]

The aspect of modular cognition that I am mainly concerned with is the intuitive categorization of nonhuman living kinds, sometimes referred to as "folk biology."[12] Even very young infants tend to assign plants and animals (including ones they have never actually encountered) to hierarchical and mutually exclusive classes. These classificatory structures seem to be applied much more readily to nonhuman living kinds than to other types of subject matter. Moreover, the boundaries of these elementary classes, defined at the levels of species and genera, exhibit limited variability across cultures. This capacity to organize knowledge of the natural world into sophisticated categories seems far in excess of what infants can absorb from environmental exposure or social learning. One explanation would be the existence of an evolved mental module for sorting living kinds into categories on the basis of morphological difference.[13] "Using verbal descriptions and pictures as inputs, the module," as Sperber and Hirschfeld note, "might build representations of many species with whom the individual is unlikely ever to interact—including extinct species such as the dinosaurs, or imaginary species such as dragons."[14]

The modularity thesis and its possible effects on cultural transmission have been extensively discussed in the work of Pascal Boyer, with primary reference to the cognitive foundations of religion.[15] Boyer argues that most anthropological studies of religion have greatly exaggerated the strange or counterintuitive aspects of religious symbolism. Representations of supernatural beings typically comprise strong elements of intuitive knowledge that appeal to modular common sense, and within which their more extraordinary characteristics are embedded. Spirits, for example, are likely to be talked about as possessing many typical attributes of persons, such as the capacity to form intentions and beliefs, despite the fact that they are mostly invisible and pass through physical obstacles. Boyer further proposes that some such cognitive balancing act is necessary for the successful transmission of religious ideas:

> In any cultural environment, indefinitely many representations of religious entities are constantly created and communicated. Only some of them, however, have the potential to support both imaginative scenarios and intuitive references. These are the ones that combine a rich intuitive base, with all its inferential potential, and a limited series of violations of intuitive theories, which are attention-demanding. Because of these characteristics, such assumptions are more likely than others

to be easily acquired, memorized, and transmitted than other assumptions. It should not be surprising, therefore, that they constitute the most recurrent aspects of religious systems.[16]

Sperber and Hirschfeld argue that representations of supernatural beings "blatantly violate the kind of basic expectations that are delivered by domain-specific cognitive mechanisms," but like Boyer they also note:

> Despite these striking departures from intuitive knowledge the appearance and behavior of supernatural beings is otherwise what intuition would expect of natural beings. That is, they have enough of the characteristic features of plants, animals, people, topographic entities or celestial bodies to fall squarely in the actual domain of cognitive modules. Supernatural animals have, apart from their supernatural features, a regular biology. . . . It is this combination of a few striking violations with otherwise conformity to ordinary expectations that makes supernatural beings attention arresting and memorable, and rich in inferential potential.[17]

Examples of "religious concepts" provided by Sperber and Boyer derive mainly from verbal statements about the behavior, thought patterns, or physical properties of supernatural agents. Such testimony is lacking for much of the material covered in this book, although textual records may flesh out the picture in some cases (as with the civilizing sea-monster of Berossos's *History of Babylonia*, in this book's epigraph). It is nevertheless consistent with an epidemiological approach to assume that the distribution of intuitive and counterintuitive characteristics may cut across multiple cognitive and sensory domains, including the visual and the tangible as well as the linguistic.[18] Indeed, the assertion that "minimally counterintuitive statements" are especially stimulating, memorable, and thus highly transmissible resonates closely with Stafford's discussion of "conspicuously interlocking images" that "change the strength of our synaptic connections since their puzzling appearance counters habituation and augments sensitization."[19]

On the expectations of this model, images of composite animals, with one foot in anatomical reality and the other in fantasy, should provide good materials for an "epidemiological" study. We might reasonably hypothesize that, as minimally counterintuitive images, they constitute robust points of reference for ideas about the supernatural, capable of crossing cultural boundaries and acting as ready vehicles for a multiplicity of ritual, theological, and mythological discourses.[20] The striking diffusion of composite figures noted by Rostovtzeff, and to be revisited in the following chapters, thus holds out the prospect of an empirical case study in the epidemiology of culture, and a step toward a cognitive history of images. As will become clear, however, things are not nearly so simple. The early history of the composite figure will ultimately oblige us to reformulate a number of the theoretical principles that have just been outlined.

COMPOSITES AND DISTRIBUTIONS

Before going any further, I want to clarify some terms of reference. I will start by explaining why, throughout the remainder of this study, I reject the term "monster" in favor of what I am calling "composites." I will then move on to explain what I mean by a "distribution of images." I use the term "images" rather than "representations," because with composites I am concerned at all times with creatures of the imagination, as opposed to pictures of living things that could be seen in the world. I will also introduce a number of comparative observations on the status of composites in the visual arts of recent hunter-gatherer societies, which offer important alternatives to assumptions about the symbolic meaning of anatomical hybrids that are ingrained in the field of cultural studies.

It may be useful to start with an evocative counterdefinition, provided by the psychologist Rudolph Arnheim in an introductory note to a book of drawings by the New York–based artist Leo Russell, published in 1949. The book bore the simple title *Monsters*. Modern art, Arnheim observed, frequently uses distortions or paradoxical combinations of images to give an impression of "man-made disorder that could and should be remedied by man." But monsters, he suggested, are uniquely disturbing images, as they alone present this disorder as "having grown naturally," as something organically formed rather than manufactured. The "birth of a monster," he suggested, represents "a failure of nature herself and threatens our faith in the basic soundness of what grows," and that is why we find "the mere thought of a biological monster so profoundly sickening," much more so than "the sight of a mutilated body."[21]

Arnheim's reading of monstrous images, vivid as it may be, is most useful here in illustrating the sort of definition that I wish to avoid, because it seems to assume so much of what should first be investigated. In fact, all that could be retained for my own purposes (were I to keep hold of the term "monster') is his description of incongruous combinations of body parts, drawn from two or more species, and forming the appearance of an organic entity. The German *Mischwesen* perhaps conveys these attributes a little more precisely. "Monster" is potentially broader. It may include beings of unnatural proportions as well as "cyborgs": living systems comprising mixtures of organic and synthetic parts. The Latin root *monstrum* further links monsters to morality, and to intimations of misfortune—portentous signs and evil omens.[22] The point was not lost on Arnheim, who talks of monsters as bearers of the "threatening message that nature can go out of joint." Interesting as all these observations may be, their main value here is to exemplify the kind of intuitive understanding of the monstrous that I am rejecting.

To retain the term "monster" for my subject matter would also risk giving an impression of Juvenalian assault upon the beliefs systems of past societies, where figures with mixed human and animal attributes may be variously associated with gods (as was the case in Egypt, for example) or protective spirits (as was usual in Mesopotamia, and known in Egypt), to be further differentiated in turn from a host of other invisible agents, such as ghosts and demons. Distinctions of this kind should of course be properly recognized and reconstructed, wherever possible, and the term "monster" is wholly inadequate in this respect.[23] Native taxonomies of supernatural agents are not, however, the main focus of this study. In many of the cases I consider, surviving source material does not permit us to attach named identities of that sort to pictures of imaginary beings. Other kinds of interpretation, more tightly focused on the internal properties of objects and images than on language or text, must be brought to bear. My preferred term of analysis, "composite," is not devoid of ambiguities. So let me be clear about what is intended.

What differentiates "composites" from other types of image? As recently highlighted by Philippe Descola, in a wide-ranging comparison of image-making traditions,[24] there is more to this question than first meets the eye. He points out that the regular production of composites implies a certain underlying approach to the rendering of body as image, which has been cultivated in many but by no means all societies.[25] The starting point for depiction is not an organism in its totality but rather its constituent elements, each of which must be accurately and realistically portrayed in its own right. Working from that principle, and subject to institutional norms and constraints, makers of images can use the various components at their disposal to assemble organic figures of different kinds, including those with clear prototypes in the visible world and those that combine elements drawn from different species. It is the latter that I refer to, throughout this study, as composites.

Precisely because of their fictive character, the creation of visually compelling composites requires *enhanced* accuracy in the depiction of individual body parts, each of which should be rendered at a common scale and should be clearly identifiable, in and of itself, as belonging to a certain kind of species. The total bodily form of that species is absent from the resulting depiction, but its presence is signified, nonetheless, by the spatial disposition of elements around a companion body that belongs to an animal of an entirely

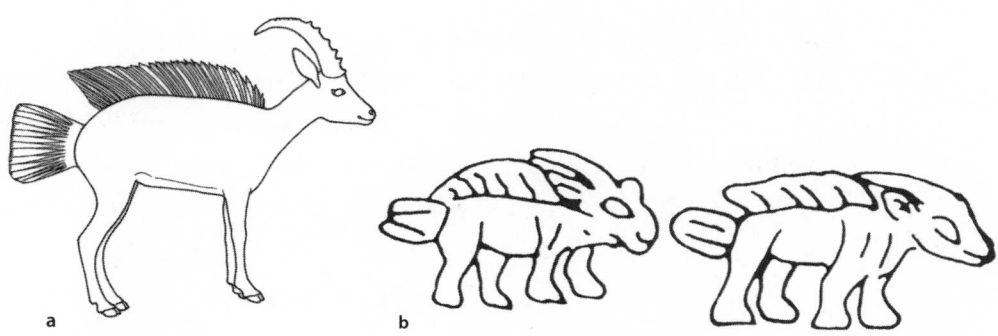

2.1. (a) Naturalistic reconstruction of (b) composite figures carved in relief on the ivory handle of a knife from Abu Zaidan, Egypt, ca. 3300 BC (see also figure 4.2; reconstruction after a drawing by F. Roloux, with permission of Dirk Huyge. © RMAH, Brussels).

different kind. The outcome is a new kind of figure that is *sui generis*, imaginary, but nevertheless retains a certain basic coherence on the anatomical plane.[26] Hence the *Tilapia* fins, on a figure from protodynastic Egypt, are placed in anatomically correct positions on a mammal's body (figure 2.1), as though it were the body of a fish; so too with the head of the Minotaur, carried on human shoulders, or the wings of Pegasus, correctly poised for flight.

As Leonardo da Vinci knew well, the visually compelling character of imaginary composites rests upon a substratum of anatomical correctness. His notebooks provide direct instructions on *How to Make an Imaginary Animal Look Natural*:

> You know that you cannot make any animal without it having limbs such that each bears some resemblance to that of some one of the other animals. If therefore you wish to make one of your imaginary animals appear natural—let us suppose it to be a dragon—take for its head that of a mastiff or setter, for its eyes those of a cat, for its ears those of a porcupine, for its nose that of a greyhound, with the eyebrows of a lion, the temples of an old cock and the neck of a water tortoise.[27]

In violating some limited part of intuitive biology, composites thus typically affirm many of its underlying structural principles. Legs are still positioned for walking, eyes for seeing, wings for flying, fins for propulsion, and so on, allowing us to infer (often extraordinary) properties of movement and vitality for the resulting figures.

IMAGE AND ONTOLOGY

Under what conditions have these particular kinds of visual experiments been either avoided or cultivated? Under what circumstances have they become integral to the construction of more encompassing systems of knowledge and meaning? Images of the kind I have in mind are of course quite central to our modern mass culture of entertainment and commercial marketing. They play especially prominent roles in the enculturation of children. Perhaps it is this deep sense of familiarity that has led some commentators to assume their ubiquity in other cultural and historical contexts, extending back into the remote prehistory of our species. "Monsters," wrote Arnheim, "have been made in all epochs of art."[28] As I will try to show, this claim—widely rehearsed in more recent studies—is actually quite difficult to substantiate. The reality, when viewed on an archaeological timescale, is both more complex and more intriguing than it suggests. The question is one of distribution, and here again I need to qualify my terms.

The first point to make concerns the differential survival of cultural media that carry and transmit images. An object lesson in caution is provided here by the orientalizing (or, more accurately, "occidentalizing") skin tattoos and felt textiles, miraculously preserved in the frozen Iron Age tombs of Pazyryk, some 1,600 meters above sea level on the High Altai, which feature a range of fantastical creatures (figure 2.2).[29] Visual media of this kind were common in earlier times too, but are not normally preserved in the archaeological record owing to their perishable nature. What we are seeing in any period is a fraction of what existed—and specifically that fraction that, through a

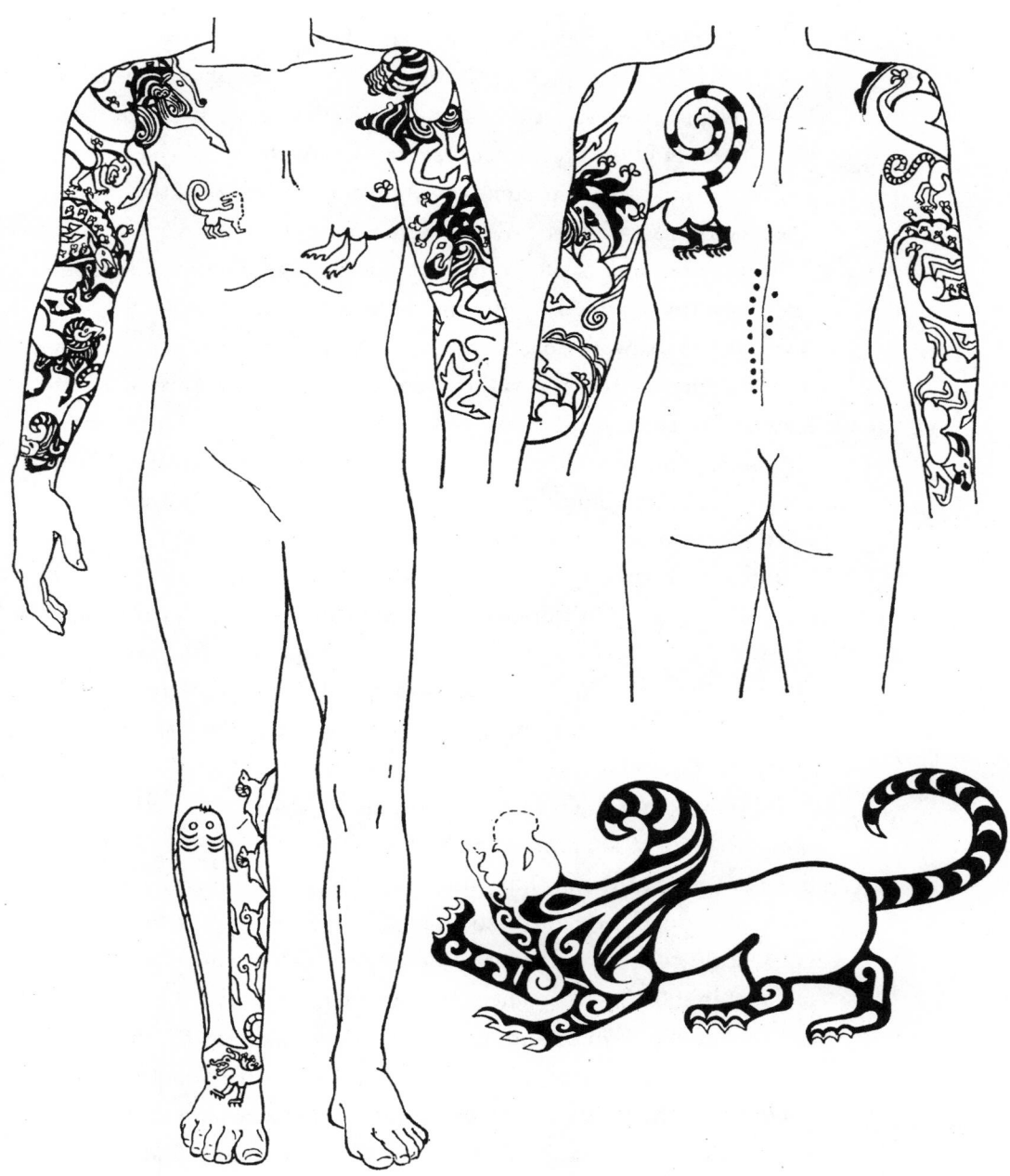

2.2. Tattooing on the body in Pazyryk *kurgan* 2, and detail from right arm, fourth century BC (after S. I. Rudenko. 1970. *Frozen Tombs of Siberia: The Pazyryk Burials of Iron Age Horsemen.* London: J. M. Dent & Sons, figs. 51–52, 128).

combination of physical durability and depositional circumstances, has survived into the present. It may not be necessary to go as far as David Napier, who suggests that we are dealing at all times with objects "that are known to us because they are made of durable materials, not because they represent any enduring categories of thought."[30] The basic observation is, however, an important one.

Further reminders of the importance of organic and perishable materials are provided by the indigenous arts of areas such as the American Northwest Coast, Amazonia, central and northern Australia, sub-Saharan Africa, and the circumpolar North. Figures made of feather, fur, sinew, and string; richly colored paintings on tree bark and skin; ornamented masks and containers of bone, wood, and ivory—these are among the mainstays of visual cultures that developed on, or beyond, the margins of agrarian states, kingdoms, and empires, with their generally more durable and monumental traditions of display. Anthropological studies of visual cultures that lie outside the canonical subject matter of art history also pose questions concerning the mixing of anatomical forms that are unlikely to arise from within our own experience, rooted as they are in other ontological frameworks.

While I do not intend to labor this latter point, it is worth noting that the kind of anatomical reshuffling, which is necessary to produce images of the sort I am interested in, seems generally quite at odds with the plastic and visual arts of recent hunter-gatherers and small-scale cultivators.[31] It is, by contrast, an extremely important element in their "performance arts," where ritual actors take on attributes of animal bodies—not (*contra* Arnheim) as signs of "disorder" or "nature gone out of joint"—but to gain a deeper empathy and insight into the thoughts of nonhuman beings whose modes of reasoning are considered similar to those of people. It also finds a place in negative sorcery, as with the Greenland Inuit practice of arranging bones from diverse species to make a temporary effigy known as *tupilak*, which served as a ritual attractor for malevolent, supernatural forces that could be sent to wreak havoc on a human victim (figure

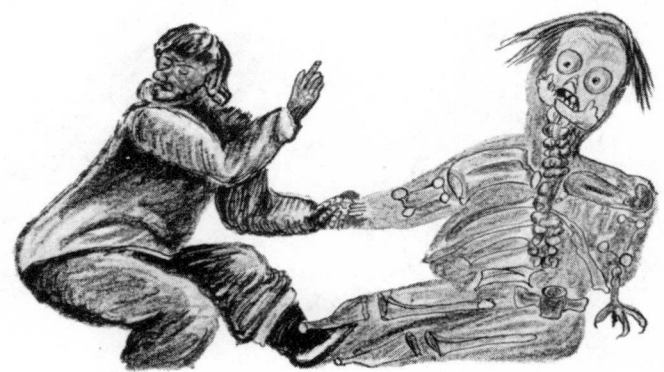

2.3. "Making a tupilak" (after K. Rasmussen. 1921. *Eskimo Folk-Tales, with Illustrations by Native Eskimo Artists*, ed. and trans. W. Worster. London and Copenhagen: Christiana, Gyldendal).

2.3). For reasons of prudence, such effigies were not traditionally rendered as permanent images.[32]

Among the Inuit, and some Amazonian and southern African groups, crossing the body boundaries that ordinarily separate one species from another is a craft or skill that all people can master, and in which some excel. These gifted individuals approximate in their abilities the tricksters and shape-shifters that indigenous folklore so often associates with a primordial age, before the world of living things was divided into the species we see around us. The success of the trickster or shaman in crossing those boundaries and navigating a safe return resides precisely in the capacity to move seamlessly between different morphological states without being caught in the process. In San legend, this quality is epitomized in the figure of the Mantis, who fools the children by taking on the appearance of a dead hartebeest, which then evades capture by regrouping its dismembered body parts in the form of a running man, and chases them home.[33] Or in the realm of material culture, we might think of the multilayered masks of the Nuxalk, Tlingit, and Kwakiutl (figure 2.4), which flicker open and shut during ritual performances, affording glimpses of a human face/being lodged within an animal body, but never more than glimpses.[34]

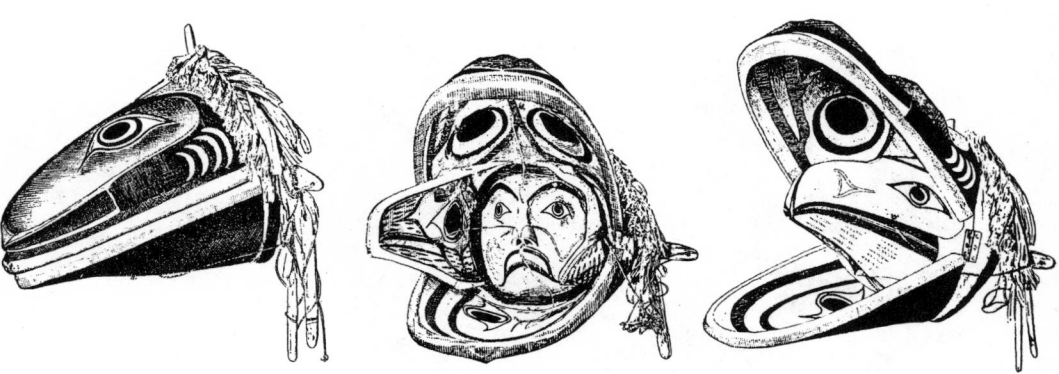

2.4. Kwakiutl multilayered mask, painted wood with hinge mechanism (after F. Boas. 1909. *The Kwakiutl of Vancouver Island.* Leiden: E. J. Brill; New York: G. E. Stechert).

To depict such states of mediation in durable form is at odds with an ontology in which fluidity and flexibility are everything, and may invite danger by leaving open a permanent trace of a relationship between human and "other" that should be properly circumscribed by rites of passage and closure. Images of composite beings, rigid and unchanging, evoke these principles of metamorphosis only to subvert them, by fixing transformations within stable forms that are capable of being repeated and disseminated, over and over again.[35] But I am getting ahead of myself. At this stage, I may be reasonably accused of having put the cart before the horse. Have I not simply assumed that Rostovtzeff's intuition was correct, and that a study of the kind proposed should begin in the Near East, and no earlier than the origins of urban life? My task in the next chapter must therefore be to consider in some detail the case for a much earlier beginning to the composite's tale, among the hunter-gatherers and villagers of remote prehistory.

THE HIDDEN SHAMAN

FICTIVE ANATOMY IN PALEOLITHIC AND NEOLITHIC ART

It has been suggested on more than one occasion that "imaginary animals, 'monsters', and composite figures are found throughout the Upper Paleolithic art tradition" that flourished among hunter-gatherers of the last Ice Age, between around 40,000 and 10,000 years ago.[1] That tradition, or better complex of traditions, is most richly documented across a broad swath of southern Europe, on what were then the fringes of a vast steppe bordering the zone of maximum glaciation. Notable concentrations of Paleolithic imagery have been discovered in the French Périgord, in Cantabrian Spain, in the Swabian Jura, and on the Russian Plain. To the east of this distribution, they are mainly restricted to mobile objects with carved surface ornament—such as hunting tools, personal ornaments, and figurines in bone and ivory—while to the west, by no later than 13,000 BC, such objects are accompanied by spectacular paintings and engraving on rock surfaces.[2]

ORIGINS OF FICTIVE ANATOMY: PALEOLITHIC ART AND RITUAL

The presence, among this surviving corpus, of figures combining human and animal attributes plays an important role in recent debates over the significance of image making among early human populations.[3] Among the earliest known is the so-called lion-man, a figure almost eleven inches high, reconstructed from fragments of mammoth ivory found toward the rear of a shallow cave at Hohlenstein Stadel, in the Lone Valley of southwest Germany (figure 3.1a).[4] Dated by its associated archaeological deposits to around 30,000 years ago, it is among the oldest examples of mobile figural sculpture in the world.[5] A still older sculpture of a standing figure has been unearthed from Hohle Fels, in the nearby Ach Valley.[6] Despite its fragmentary state, comparisons have been drawn with the lion-man; but alternative interpretations of both figures remain possible.[7]

A clearer example of a figure with mixed human and animal attributes appears on an engraved plaque found at Etiolles, in the Paris Basin, positioned behind a carving of a horse (figure 3.1c).[8] Dated to around 12,000 years ago, it belongs to the final stages of the Upper Paleolithic, as the last major phase of glacial climate was drawing to a close. The special nature of this object is further indicated by its archaeological context. It was found face down, and seemingly deliberately hidden, beneath a supporting block of a prehistoric hearth. Of similar, or slightly earlier, date is the carved and painted image often referred to as the "Sorcerer," found deep within a network of subterranean passages at Les Trois Frères, in the Ariège uplands of southern France. The original was probably executed around 14,000 years ago, but the image that still features in most scholarly and popular publications was created by the Abbé Henri Breuil in the early twentieth century (figure 3.1b).[9]

Breuil, whose copies of prehistoric rock art have been widely influential, followed the interpretive paradigm that was prevalent in his day.[10] This emphasized the magical role of animal images in increasing the fertility of herds and the success of hunting, a view now widely rejected in light of the lack of correspondence between species most commonly depicted in cave paintings (such as bison, horses, and mammoth), and those whose physical remains are most frequently reported from habitation sites (notably reindeer). The conditions under which Breuil recorded rock art were often, by his own admission, difficult, and some of the techniques used were at best simple. In the case of Les Trois Frères, a period of twenty years

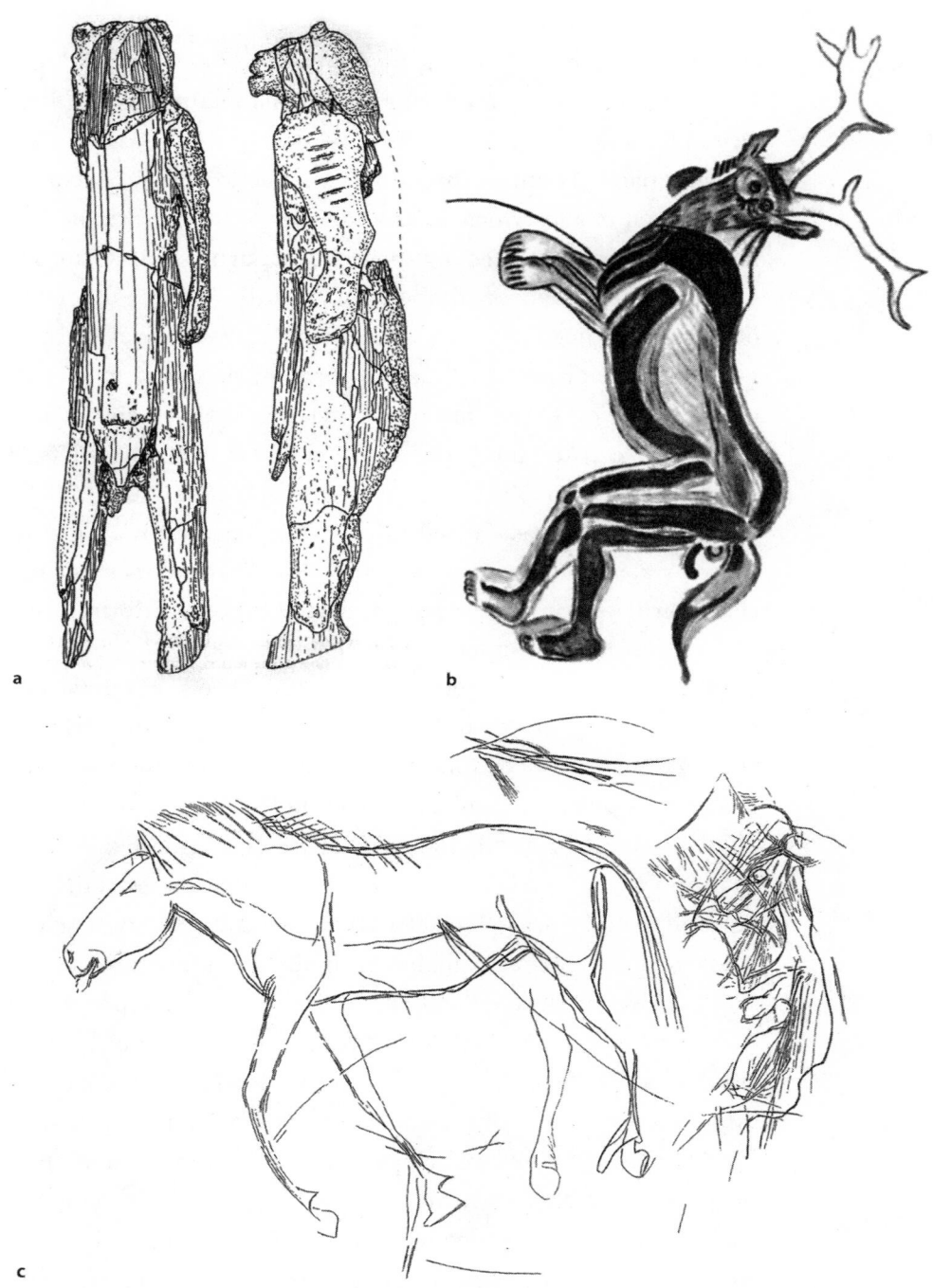

3.1. (a) Ivory statuette from Hohlenstein-Stadel, Germany, ca. 30,000 BC; (b) the Abbé Henri Breuil's rendering of a carved and painted figure known as the "Sorcerer" from Les Trois-Frères cave, France, ca. 12,000 BC; and (c) engraved plaque from Etiolles, France, ca. 10,000 BC (after Hahn 1986, p. 247, pl. 17; Breuil 1952, p. 166, fig. 130; Taborin et al. 2001, p. 126, fig. 2).

elapsed between the making of the copies and their publication, which often involved redrawing by a collaborator who had never visited the caves.[11]

Discrepancies between Breuil's reconstruction of the Sorcerer and the original image, which lacks a number of the features he identified, were already pointed out some decades ago.[12] Reservations have sometimes been expressed about the identification of other Paleolithic images, deemed to represent imaginary creatures or masked humans.[13] Nevertheless, these figures remain central to recent interpretations of Paleolithic image making. David Lewis-Williams, for example, takes the presence of hybrid human-animal figures, or masked human figures, as support for his theory that much Paleolithic rock art was created as part of shamanic rituals involving altered states of consciousness, whereby human actors entered into close participation with ancestral spirits in animal form.[14] Steven Mithen considers whether the much earlier creation of figures such as the lion-man might reflect a fundamental change in human cognition, taking place around 30,000 years ago or perhaps earlier still, and signaling the inception of a dual capacity for complex symbolizing and sophisticated social interaction.[15]

The prominence ascribed to such figures in interpretation is out of all proportion to their quantity. During the later phases of the Upper Paleolithic (ca. 13,000–10,000 BC), when archaeological traces of image making are first available in significant quantities, the record is dominated by detailed and anatomically accurate representations of living kinds: large mammals as well as smaller, but significant numbers of birds, fish, and (mainly female) humans. Among this extensive corpus of painted and engraved figures, it has proved difficult to identify images of beings with composite anatomies that are replicated with any degree of fidelity. Suggestions to the contrary are often bolstered by selective comparisons with the rock art of living or recent hunter-gatherers in southern Africa.[16] In fact, such images are far from ubiquitous there, and their chronological range is unknown.[17] Were we, in spite of this, to admit the more regular depiction of composites or masked human actors in recent rock art traditions, this would surely provide an instructive point of contrast, rather than a surrogate for the Paleolithic record.

Questioning the frequency of composites among the surviving corpus of Paleolithic art does not, of course, require us to postulate that its creators had anything other than fully modern minds, capable of communicating complex symbolic messages. Nor does it require us to reject interpretations that explore the significance of such images in the ritual life of prehistoric societies. It does, however, establish an important benchmark for studying their distribution in the archaeological record. The significant point, to which I will return, is that if such beings did populate the collective imaginary of early hunter-gatherers, then their presence was made manifest predominantly through ephemeral modes of display such as psychotropic visions and masked performances that have left few durable traces.

In searching for more positive evidence of such displays, we are obliged to probe below the surface of the land into the funerary record of Paleolithic and Mesolithic societies, with their often effusive ritual compositions of human and animal body parts (figure 3.2). Examples can be traced far back in time from the "shamanic" graves of later prehistory[18] to the much older cross-species burials of the Carmel caves; the latter, dating to around 100,000 BC, bringing us almost to the dawn of the human story.[19] But these ritual composites, which will remain an important feature of Neolithic funerary customs,[20] find only the faintest of echoes in the surviving visual record. Perhaps there is something to be learned from that silence, about the limits set by early hunter-gatherers to the materialization of the invisible?

IMAGERY OF THE FIRST FARMERS

At what point in the archaeological record do durable images of composite beings achieve some wider currency? We might look with some optimism to the much more diverse record of Neolithic art.

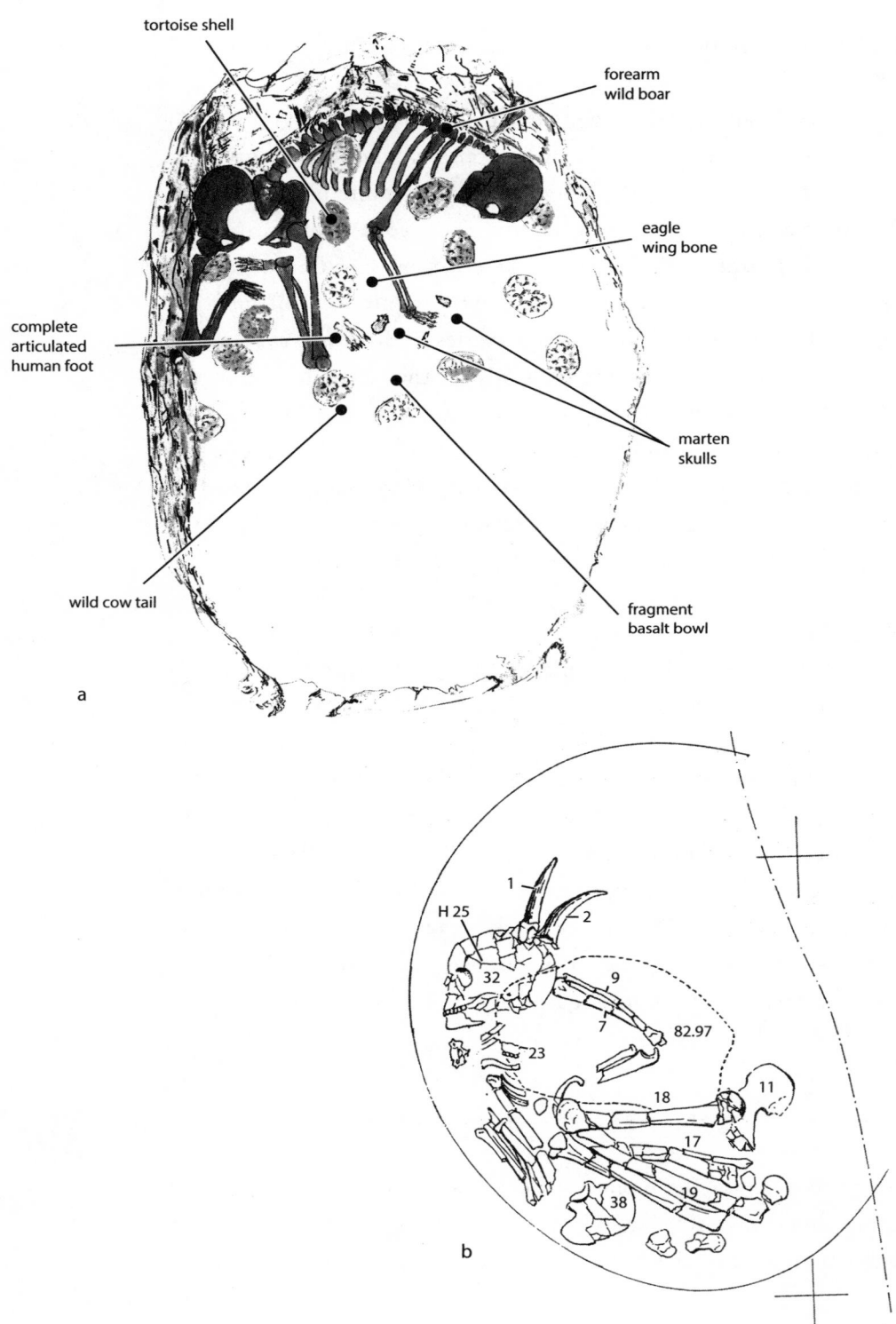

tortoise shell

forearm
wild boar

eagle
wing bone

complete
articulated
human foot

marten
skulls

wild cow tail

fragment
basalt bowl

a

H 25

1

2

32

9

7

23

82.97

18

11

17

19

38

b

In doing so, my focus will be upon areas that would subsequently witness the emergence of the earliest cities and states. Those same regions of the Near East and northeast Africa have produced unusually dense concentrations of late prehistoric imagery, distributed across a wide range of media, and allowing us the privilege of a diachronic perspective on the millennia between the end of the last Ice Age (ca. 10,000 BC) and the beginnings of urban life (ca. 4000 BC).[21]

The period in question saw the domestication of cereal crops and herd animals, and the establishment of sedentary life across a significant part of the western Old World.[22] In an influential study, Jacques Cauvin characterized these developments as "the birth of the gods and the origins of agriculture."[23] He was referring to a series of pronounced changes in ritual and symbolic expression that accompanied the early stages of plant and animal domestication in western Asia, and then spread—together with the farming economy—to neighboring regions. At the core of Cauvin's argument was a contention that Neolithic representations of supernatural agency differed from those of earlier, hunter-gather societies. He perceived in the symbolism of the first farming communities an acknowledgment of remote and invisible deities: a new register of divinity, dominating and mastering a preexisting order of relations between humans and ancestral beings. With the "birth of the gods," those ancestral figures formerly credited with the making of the cosmos were relegated to a lower plane of reality, closer to the material world of ordinary humanity. Hence, Neolithic villages became populated by the physical remains of human and animal ancestors, impinging on the most intimate spaces of the household, making new and complex demands upon the society of the living. Among those demands, we find the

3.2. Mixed burials of human and animal body parts from sites of the Natufian period in Israel, ca. 10,000 BC: (a) elderly woman with fifty tortoise shells and parts of wild boar, eagle, cow, leopard, and martens, from Hilazon Tachtit (image by P. Groszman, from Grosman et al. 2008; courtesy L. Grosman); (b) adult (?)female with disarranged body parts and gazelle horn-cores, from Mallaha (Eynan; after Perrot and Ladiray 1988, fig. 32).

performance of labor-intensive rituals, which involved the cleansing and symbolic refleshing of skulls, and the provision of exotic materials—pigments, shells, and colored stones—which ornamented the bodies of both the living and the dead.

To what extent can this Neolithic birth of the gods also be considered a "birth of monsters," or rather "composites," to be precise? Was it among these societies, unprecedented in their willingness to intervene in the reproductive patterns of other species, that anatomical hybrids made a concerted entry to the world of images? The existence of such images among the surviving corpus of Neolithic pictorial art has been quite widely discussed,[24] but in fact remains intriguingly difficult to substantiate.[25] Among the few archaeologists to comment directly on this point is Klaus Schmidt, the excavator of Göbekli Tepe, a ceremonial center of the ninth millennium BC, located between the mountains and plains of southeast Turkey and within the broad zone where changes in hunter-gatherer lifestyles were under way that would lead, within a few centuries, to the adoption of farming.[26]

A rich assemblage of monumental relief carvings and freestanding sculpture was built into the stone architecture of this remarkable site. The figures, a selection of which are illustrated in figure 3.3, include an array of wild animals, such as lion and boar, some with a ferocious, almost nightmarish aspect. While bodies were often schematically rendered, faces were carved in some detail. Open mouths contain lolling tongues and carefully depicted rows of gnashing teeth: features that, even in royal hunting scenes, seem to have been avoided by the makers of much later urban monuments in the same region. Certain carvings, notably that of a bird that appears to sit and manipulate a round object, may ascribe human-like motor skills to animals. Others, such as the figure of a bull, are rendered in twisted perspective, with the body depicted in profile and the head as if seen from above. There is something undeniably otherworldly about this corpus of images, yet they make very little play on the possibilities of composite depiction.

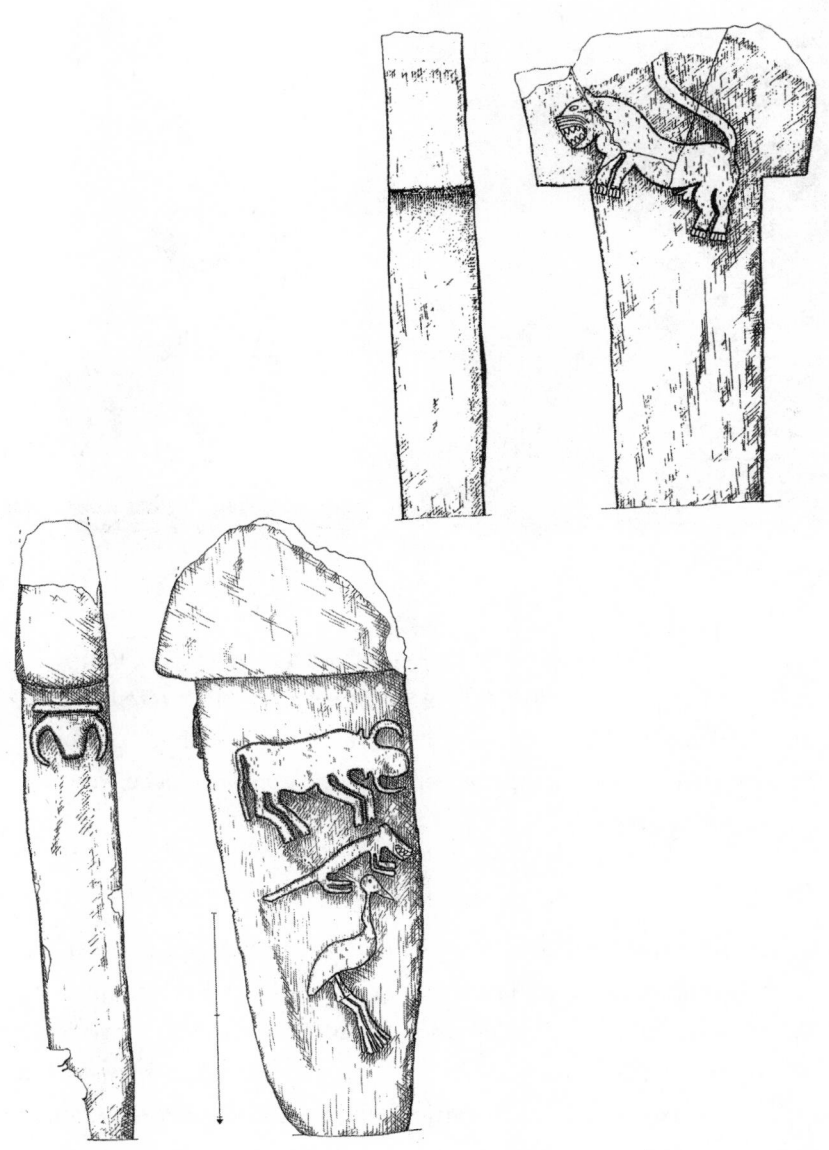

3.3. Monumental animal reliefs on stone monoliths from the Pre-Pottery Neolithic site of Gö-bekli Tepe, southeast Turkey, ca. 9000 BC (after K. Schmidt. 1998. Frühneolithische Tempel. Ein Forschungsbericht zum präkeramischen Neolithikum Obermesopotamiens. *Mitteilungen der Deutschen Orient Gesellschaft* 130: 17–49).

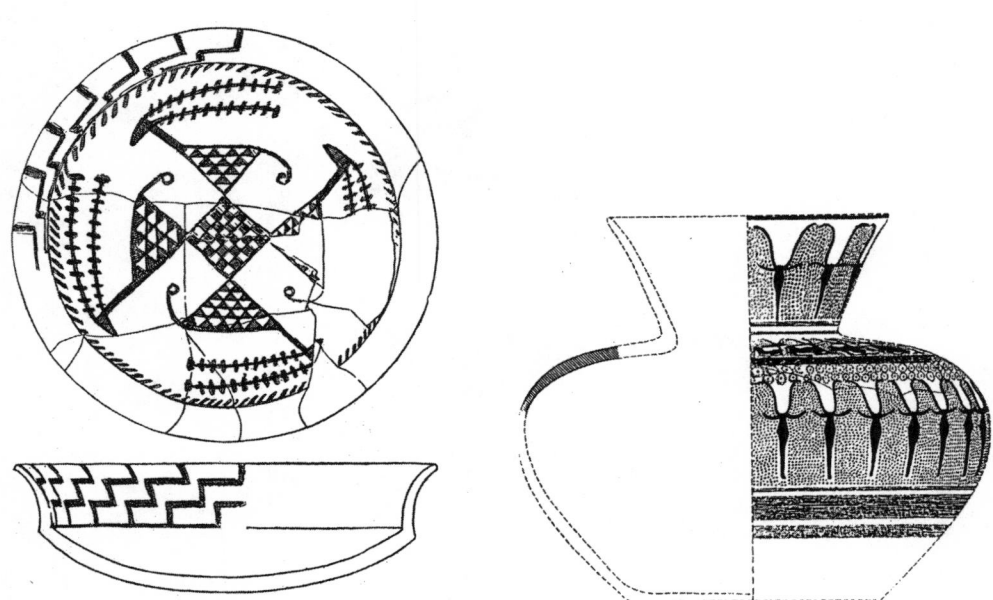

3.4. Painted ceramic containers of the Late Neolithic period with animal ornament, from Samarra (Iraq, seventh millennium BC; after E. Herzfeld. 1930. *Die vorgeschichtlichen Töpfereien von Samarra*. Berlin: Dietrich Reimer Verlag, fig. 23) and Tell Halaf (Syria, sixth millennium BC; after M. F. von Oppenheim. 1943. *Tell Halaf. Erster Band: die prähistorischen Funde*. Berlin: de Gruyter, pl. 6.2; figures not to scale).

The observation gains in interest as we broaden our horizons to neighboring regions, and to later periods of Near Eastern prehistory. Where cross-site regularities do exist in the subject matter of pictorial representation, they relate to recognizable types of wild fauna (felines, serpents, boar, and cattle), while the miniature clay figurines recovered from many sites show mainly horned ungulates and human forms, readily distinguishable from one another in the majority of cases.[27] Other popular subjects include carnivorous scavengers, perhaps reflecting their role in the ritual removal of flesh from human and animal corpses, prior to revivification with clay and other substances.[28] On the eastern mound of Çatalhöyük (ca. 7500–6000 BC), in the Konya Plain of central Turkey, there is evidence that crane wings were worn by human actors in ritual performances,[29] but compelling images of composite beings have proved difficult to identify among the site's uniquely rich corpus of mobile and parietal art.[30]

Surviving evidence for the development of pictorial art in the later Neolithic of the Near East focuses on the ornamentation of handmade serving vessels. In the seventh and sixth millennia BC, household ceramics became a preferred medium for the execution of painted designs that followed common templates across extensive networks of village societies, spanning impressive geographical distances. Right across the monochrome and polychrome traditions of these periods, painters appear to have favored the depiction of natural kinds of animal and floral subjects, especially those with obvious symmetrical properties that harmonized with the forms of vessels, themselves inspired by the structural properties of basketry (figure 3.4).[31] Similar observations can be made for the painted pottery traditions of neighboring Iran during the sixth and fifth millennia BC.[32] Composites are also hard to detect among the late Neolithic corpora of clay and stone figurines from northern Mesopotamia, which comprise either animal or human subjects, the latter depicted with widely varying degrees of schematization, and sometimes with added elements of costume or body ornamentation.[33]

Farther west, a rich and distinctive corpus of late prehistoric (or "predynastic") art, dating to the early and middle parts of the fourth millennium (ca. 4000–3300 BC), is preserved from the Nile Valley. It focuses to a greater extent upon the ornamentation of cosmetic implements such as ivory combs and palettes for the grinding of body paint (figure 3.5)—legacies from the more mobile Neolithic societies of this region, where farming economies centered initially upon herding rather than raising crops.[34] In bringing this chapter to a close I will consider the development of this predynastic art, focusing on changing methods of animal depiction and their relationship to anatomical knowledge in pictorial and nonpictorial domains. This forms a prelude to chapter 4, where I discuss the transformation of Egyptian visual culture during the period of state formation, including the introduction of composite figures, both local and externally derived.

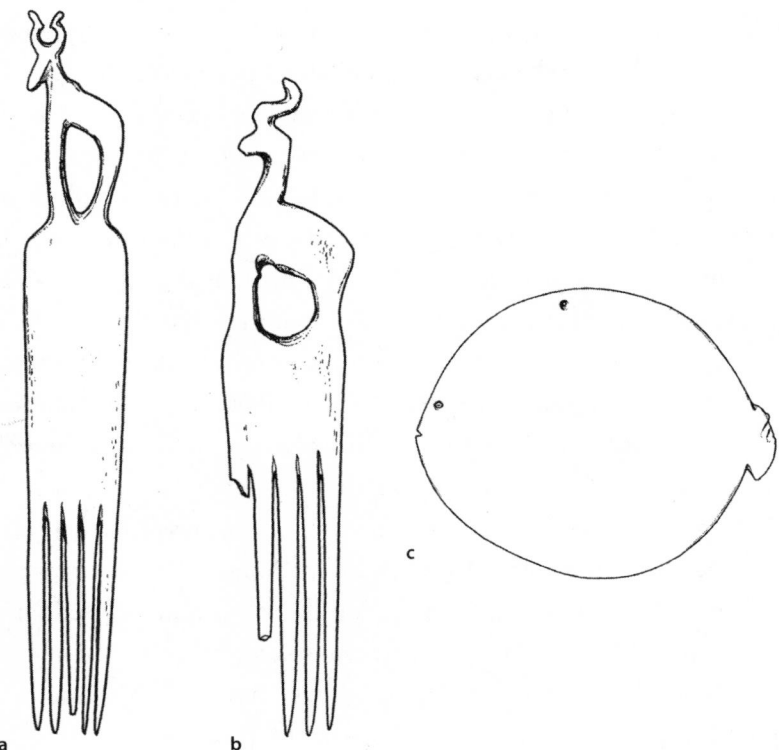

3.5. Predynastic Egyptian cosmetic articles with animal ornament, early to mid-fourth millennium BC: (a, b) bone combs from Naqada, Upper Egypt; (c) fish-shaped siltstone palette for grinding cosmetics from Tell el-Amarna (after J. C. Payne. 1993. *Catalogue of the Predynastic Egyptian Collection in the Ashmolean Museum*. Oxford, UK: Clarendon Press, figs. 75: 1839 and 77: 1904–1905; courtesy Ashmolean Museum, University of Oxford; figures not to scale).

AN ART OF AFFINITY: RELATIONALITY IN PREDYNASTIC EGYPT

In Egypt, as elsewhere, prehistoric societies existed in close proximity to the animal world. Detailed observation of animal behavior was integral to the successful pursuit of a hunter-gatherer lifestyle, evidence for which can be traced back into the deep Paleolithic record of North East Africa.[35] So too was the effective butchering of carcasses and the use of animal skins, bone, teeth and other body parts for a variety of practical and ritual purposes. Hunting remained an important activity following the widespread adoption of domestic animals in the fifth millennium BC, and later that of cereal farming in the fourth.[36] Focused attention on animal anatomy is also evident in the prehistoric funerary record. Burials of animals, both wild and domestic, are attested in Neolithic cemeteries throughout the Nile Valley, and preservative treatments were applied to animal (as well as human) corpses by no later than the mid-fourth millennium BC.[37]

At Hierakonpolis, in the south of the country, there is evidence for the curation and sacrifice of wild animals in contexts of ceremonial display. Set back from the floodplain of the Nile on the fringes of a large *wadi*, a remarkable concentration of animal burials, dating to the early and middle parts of the fourth millennium, was established around a complex of human interments partitioned by fenced enclosures.[38] They included specimens of elephant, aurochs, hippopotamus, hartebeest, baboon, dog, and wild cats.[39] Many of these species must have been brought from distant locations. Another strikingly diverse assemblage of aquatic fauna (turtle, crocodile, and perch of exceptional size) together with wild mammals (Barbary sheep, hare, gazelle) derives from a further enclosure located closer to the floodplain, within the nearby settlement.[40]

Archaeological evidence of this sort has a bearing on our understanding of contemporaneous imagery, in which animals feature prominently. It demonstrates beyond doubt that predynastic societies in Egypt cultivated intimate firsthand knowledge, not just of the species they kept as domesticates, but also of an extraordinary range of wild fauna distributed across the Nile Valley and the adjacent deserts. In addition to freestanding figurines, media on which animals (and a range of other subjects) were depicted included painted ceramics and a variety of portable, cosmetic articles such as stone palettes for the grinding of pigment and combs, pins, or spoons made of bone or ivory (see figure 3.5).[41] A painted vase (figure 3.6), one of two found within a human burial at Abydos in southern Egypt, serves to

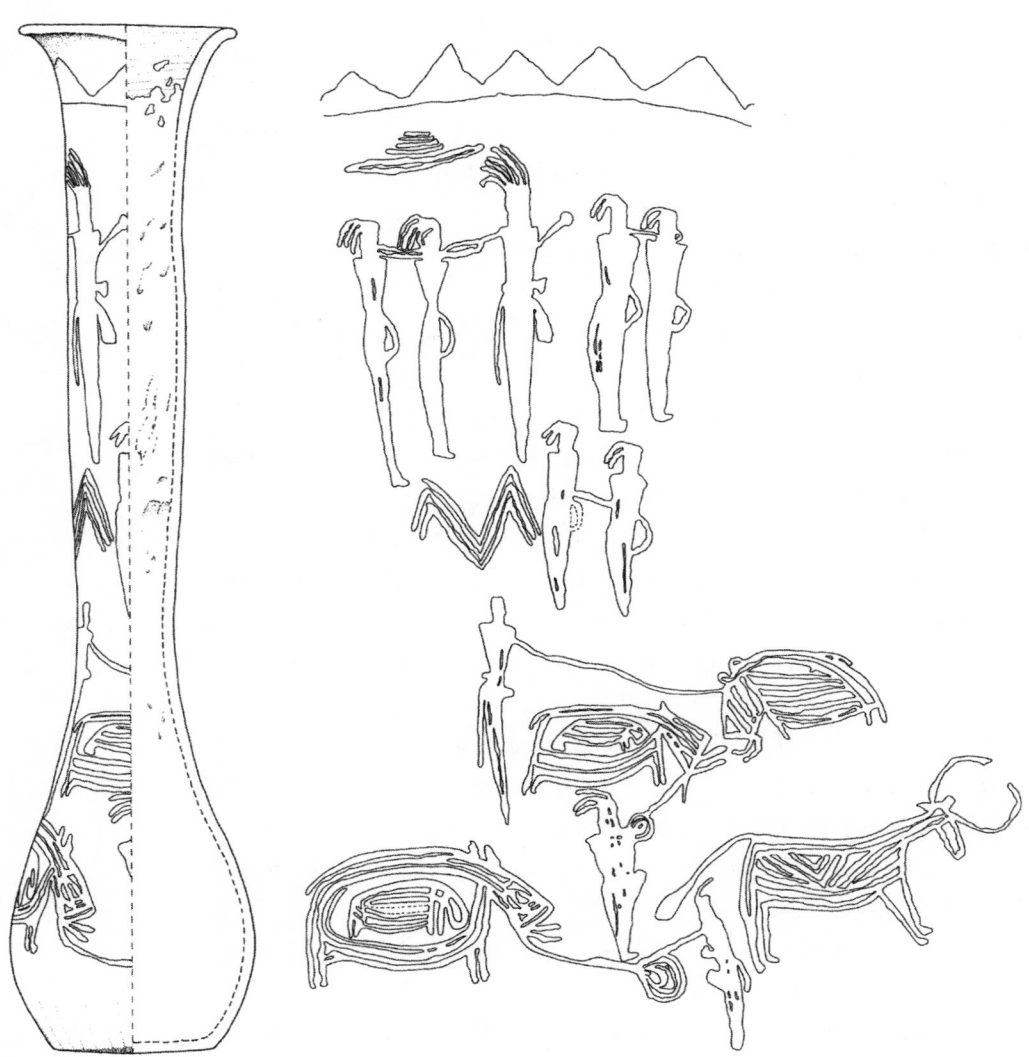

3.6. Tall vase with painted decoration (white on red burnish), from a burial at Abydos, Umm el-Qaab, Upper Egypt, early fourth millennium BC (Naqada I period; after Dreyer et al. 2003; courtesy F. Arnold, DAI Cairo).

introduce the predynastic mode of depiction for living kinds.[42] It belongs to a class of red-polished ceramics, decorated in white with linear designs, that were regularly produced between around 4000 and 3650 BC.[43] The painters of such vessels, which also included bowls and beakers, usually filled the bodies of animals with linear patterns such as radiating triangles, diamonds, or cross-hatching, and on any given container those patterns varied consistently between species. On the taller Abydos vase, the depiction of baby hippo in the bellies of larger ones suggests a concern with what is inside animals, and therefore invisible, which may be relevant to an understanding of nonfigural body patterning as well.

Relationships between the internal contents of figures and the wider "landscape" in which they appear are also suggested by the extension of filling patterns and motifs from animal bodies to surrounding parts of the container.[44] Human forms, by contrast, are often painted almost solid. Scale and outline provide the only axes of differentiation among them. Their relationships to one another, and also to animals, are indicated by schematic lines, which may or may not represent real objects such as limbs or ropes.[45] On a later type of painted pottery, produced between ca. 3650–3300 BC,[46] solid color—now painted dark on a pale, marl ceramic—was often used to fill the bodies of both humans and animals completely. As on the earlier painted pottery, elements of costume and the objects carried by humans appear as further extensions of an overall body-shape.[47]

Despite this lack of emphasis on anatomical detail, animal figures on predynastic pottery of both painted varieties take generally realistic and identifiable forms. Clear and bold outlines allow them to be identified as species existing on the Nile floodplain or in the surrounding low deserts. Contemporaneous images on other media, such as palettes and combs, can for the most part be similarly identified as turtles, birds, fish, hippopotami, horned mammals, and so on.[48] In certain cases, however, a play on visual resemblances seems calculated to elicit more than one possible identification, or to avoid definitive identification altogether. A widely distributed type of pendant—found mainly in infant burials—can thus be equally well identified with a bull, ram, or elephant head (figure 3.7a).[49] Similar ambiguities surround the interpretation of certain animal designs on cosmetic implements. Combs, pins, and grinding palettes are often

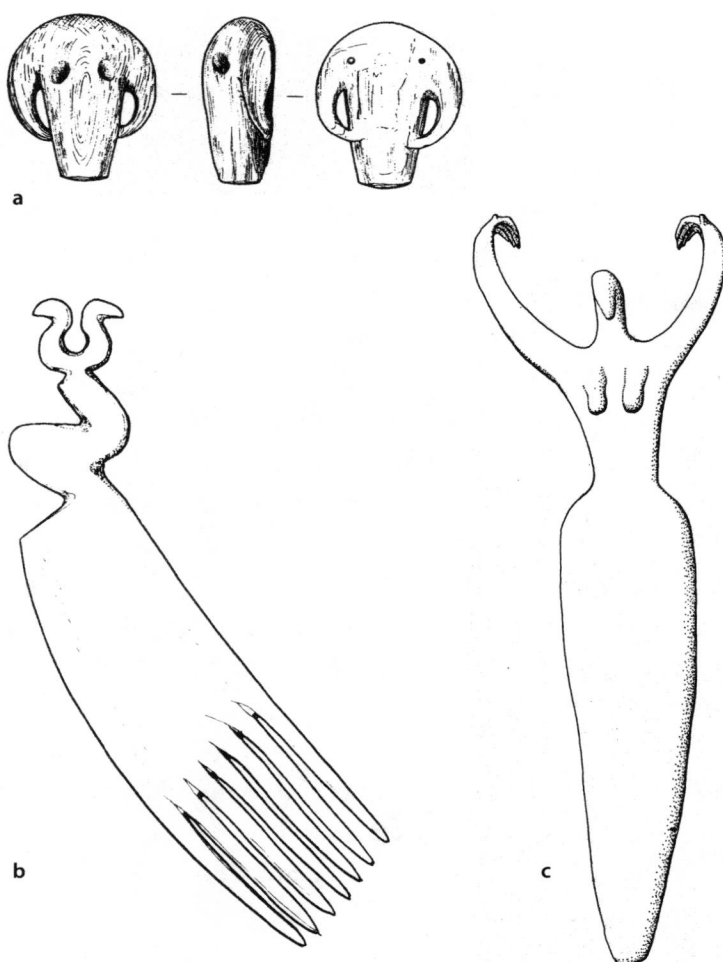

3.7. Ambiguous forms in predynastic Egyptian art, early fourth millennium BC: (a) ivory pendant and (b) bone comb from burials at Naqada (after Payne 1993; figures courtesy Ashmolean Museum, University of Oxford), and (c) clay figurine from el-Ma'amariya (courtesy J. Hubert; figures not to scale).

topped with symmetrical extensions that have been variously identified as horns or opposed bird-heads (figure 3.7b).[50] Some anthropomorphic figurines have beak-like faces, and a striking group from el-Ma'amariya includes figures with arms raised in a posture that might be identified with curving horns or outstretched wings (figure 3.7c).[51]

Insofar as these latter images combine aspects of different body forms, it is in a manner clearly distinct from the composite figures that we find associated with gods and demons in later dynastic art, and whose beginnings I will discuss in the chapter that follows. The earlier, predynastic hybrids do not result from a systematic division and recombination of standardized body parts. Instead they seem to arise from a thoughtful play on continuities and resemblances in the appearance of various species, resulting in a mode of depiction that continues to resist modern attempts at classification. They belong not to the urbanized image world of the composite figure, where we will shortly arrive, but to an earlier art of ambiguity where the forms of living beings mingle and interpenetrate on contact, and where meaningful relations emerge from the blending of affinities rather than from the assemblage of contrasts.

4

URBAN CREATIONS

THE CULTURAL ECOLOGY OF COMPOSITE ANIMALS

In chapter 1, I retraced Mikhail Rostovtzeff's search for the origins of "animal style" art in the ancient Old World. There he drew attention to the distinctive pattern-forming behavior of composite figures in the visual record. Despite appearing to be acts of free association, imaginary beings of this type turn out to share formal characteristics that recur frequently and consistently between societies. In the course of the Bronze and Iron Ages, they achieved impressive distributions that extend widely across cultural and political boundaries: a case of cultural resilience against apparently surprising odds (see the following, and chapters 5 and 6).

To explain the peculiar resilience and "catchiness" of composite animals, I laid out, in chapter 2, a preliminary hypothesis based on the principles of evolutionary psychology, and in particular the "epidemiology of culture." I explored ways in which existing models of that sort might be extended from the analysis of language to images. In particular, I considered how—by targeting our intuitive faculties for the perception of living kinds, but also introducing a breach of expectations—images of composite animals might approximate the cognitive effects of "minimally counterintuitive" propositions, of a kind widely discussed in the evolutionary psychology of religion. Provided the correct balance is achieved, and the ratio of real to unreal elements does not tip too far either way, an epidemiological model would attribute to such images certain selective advantages, accounting for their ability to become "both relatively stable within a group and recurrent among different groups."[1]

The patchiness of composites in the prehistoric visual record, which I discussed in the preceding chapter, has already posed difficulties for this hypothesis. It is beyond doubt that Paleolithic and Neolithic societies sometimes created durable images of composite beings, and the few surviving candidates have often been accorded great prominence in modern interpretations. Yet they remain strikingly isolated. If the popularity of minimally counterintuitive images is to be explained by their core cultural content and its appeal to universal cognitive biases, then why did composite figures fail so spectacularly to "catch on" across the many millennia of innovation in visual culture that precede the onset of urban life? Much hinges here upon our conceptualization of the "counterintuitive" and its role in cultural transmission, a problem that I will return to in later chapters. A more immediate priority is to establish the point at which such figures *do* achieve some wider currency, and begin to behave in the kind of culturally contagious ways that Rostovtzeff would have recognized for later antiquity. To what kind of "cultural ecology"[2] does the composite animal belong? In answering this question, I will begin where the previous chapter left off, in Egypt.

FITNESS OR "FITTINGNESS"? COMPOSITES IN EARLY DYNASTIC EGYPT

It has long been recognized that the emergence of a unified territorial state in Egypt, between around 3300 and 3000 BC, was accompanied by marked transformations in visual culture.[3] The change is most apparent in the development of images that were carved in raised relief on ceremonial objects of the period. Such objects, which include weapons and items of personal display, express the self-fashioning practices of ascendant elites.[4] Dense arrangements of figures emerge directly from their surfaces, like magnified versions of the raised impressions produced by cylinder seals. The latter were introduced to Egypt from western Asia around the middle of the fourth millennium BC[5] as a novel way of marking the clay closures of

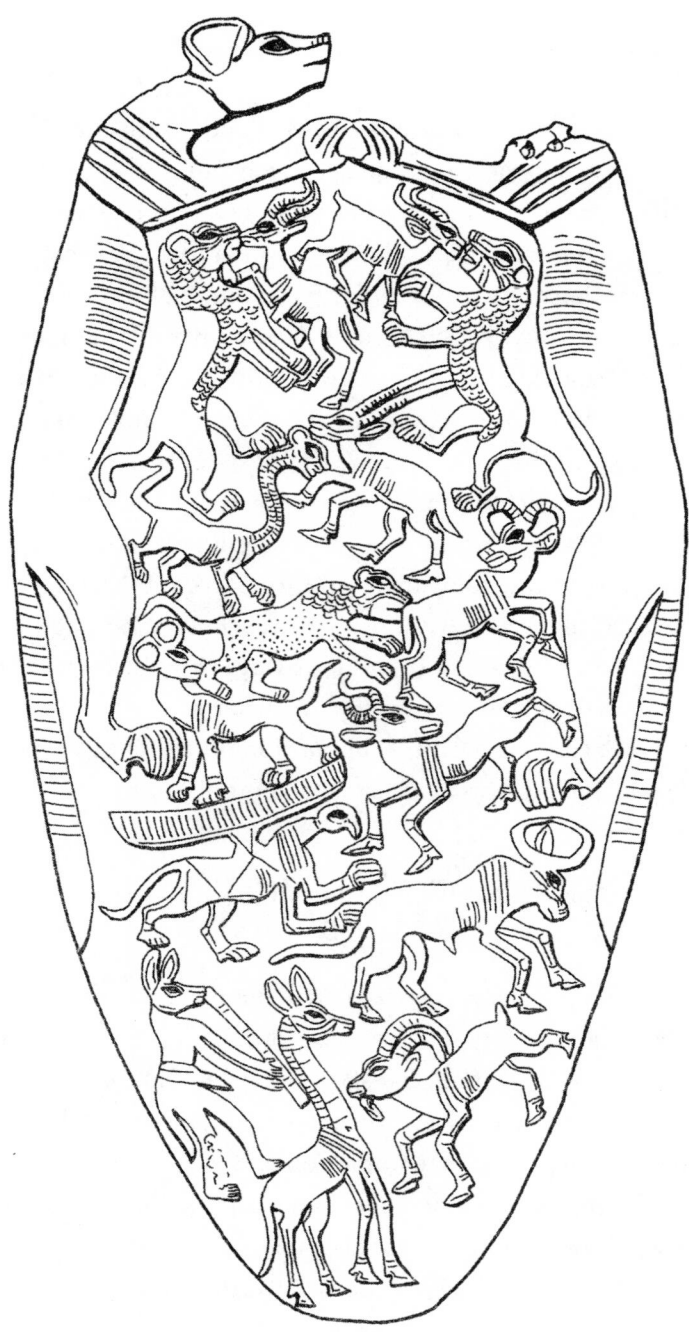

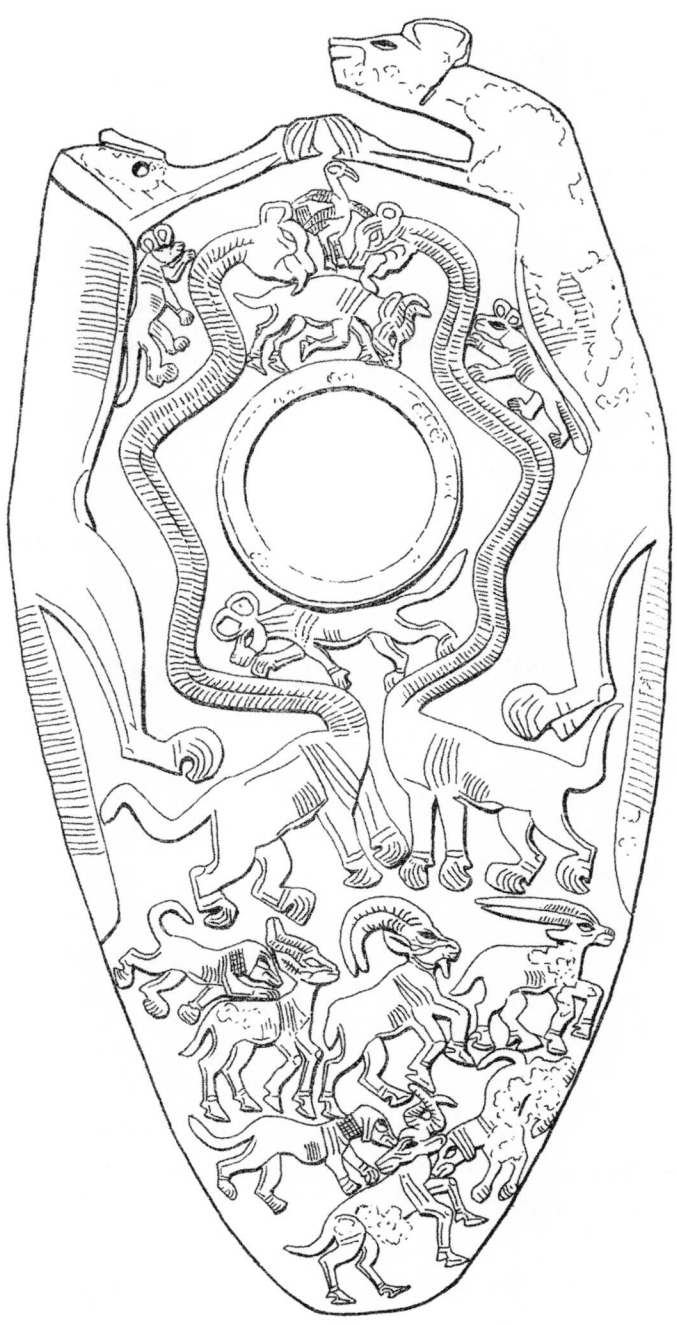

4.1. The "Two Dog Palette" from Hierakonpolis, Upper Egypt, ca. 3200 BC (courtesy Ashmolean Museum, University of Oxford; drawing by Marion Cox).

commodity vessels, including vessels deposited as offerings in high status tombs. At that time, competing chiefdoms reached out to obtain novel sources of distinction and prestige, forming new frontiers of exchange around the Levantine coast and the shores of the Arabian Peninsula.[6]

Periods of intensified exposure to outside influence are often also times of extraordinary cultural efflorescence and innovation, combined with aggressive competition over traditional sources of value. In Egypt, investment in new modes of depiction focused initially upon established status symbols and media of personal presentation. Cosmetic grinding palettes, combs, knives, and mace-heads—central components of social display in the Nile Valley since Neolithic times—were now decorated with relief figures of wild and dangerous animals (figure 4.1).[7] Both in technical execution and principles of composition, these sculpted bodies mark a departure from the animal imagery of predynastic times, discussed in chapter 3. Together with the novel play on light and shadow produced by relief carving, there is a completely new emphasis on details of joints and musculature. Once the outline of a figure had been established, incision and fine modeling were used to distinguish not only individual body parts but also particular structural features and elements that correspond to an empirical reality below the skin. In some cases, the repetitive carving of these lifelike creations in row after minute row suggests an aesthetic interest in the standardization of form (figure 4.2). The Egyptian (dynastic) artist, as Kent Weeks suggests: "was a keen observer of nature and, even in the earliest reliefs he exhibited an awareness of the subtleties of musculature and surface anatomy to the point that some of his relief figures look like illustrations from an early medical textbook."[8]

These observations should, however, be set against the pervasive unreality of protodynastic Egyptian art. The same anatomical empiricism that allows these animal depictions to be identified with zoological precision[9] also produced an entirely new kind of visual imaginary, based on the subdivision of accurately rendered body

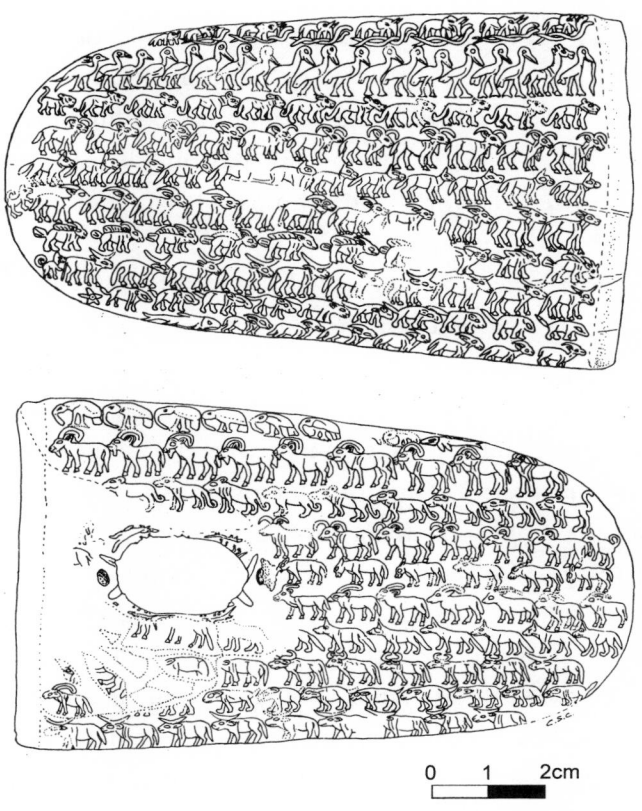

4.2. Ivory handle of a ceremonial flint knife found at Abu Zaidan, Upper Egypt, ca. 3300 BC (after Needler 1984; drawings by C. S. Churcher; courtesy Brooklyn Museum, Museum Collection Fund, New York).

parts and their reassembly into ostentatiously artificial wholes. It is as though the entire field of image making were being reinvented on the basis of a new theory of material connections and integration; a new understanding of part–whole relations, of which composite animals—which now included both homegrown and imported varieties[10]—are just one, especially clear manifestation. The same applies, broadly, to dynastic modes of depiction for the human form, the core principles of which remained relatively stable from the First Dynasty onward. Bodies were constructed out of standardized parts, each depicted with great precision in its typical form and assembled in the manner of a "composite diagram."[11] Anatomical elements were treated almost as discrete entities, unified within the confines of an encompassing outline. Their dimensions adhered broadly, but not rigidly, to an ideal system of proportions, compatible with more general principles of Egyptian metrology.[12]

This modular logic of depiction provided a powerful template for integrating art and writing, and for the close translation of forms between two- and three-dimensional surfaces.[13] Phonetic or ideographic signs could thus be mounted on legs, endowed with arms, or enclosed within architectural motifs to enhance their meaning within a composition (figure 4.3a). "Composite hieroglyphs" of this kind are attested in a variety of forms by the First Dynasty, and may have been initially developed for the writing of royal names.[14] They were integral to the formation of the dynastic representational system as a whole. Statuary, and in particular the cult statues of gods, is likely to have formed the core of that system, providing models for royal and elite display.[15] Two-dimensional and relief representations of divine agency, which survive in greater numbers, include (but are not confined to) figures that fuse an idealized human body with an animal head. Composites of the latter sort were not depictions of gods. Rather they extended the visual logic of the hieroglyphic system to beings whose true physicality was unknown, and who could therefore be approached only through allusions to their supposed qualities and functions.[16] A host of "demonic" agents, both benevolent and harmful, were also approached through images of composite bodies, depicted on magically protective instruments and texts (figure 4.3b).[17]

Intriguingly, the adoption of composite principles in Egyptian art was accompanied by analogous developments in a range of other technological domains, especially those associated with the activities of the early dynastic court (ca. 3100–2800 BC), attested mainly in the material remains of elaborate funerary rituals. Modular construction techniques can be detected in both miniature and monumental

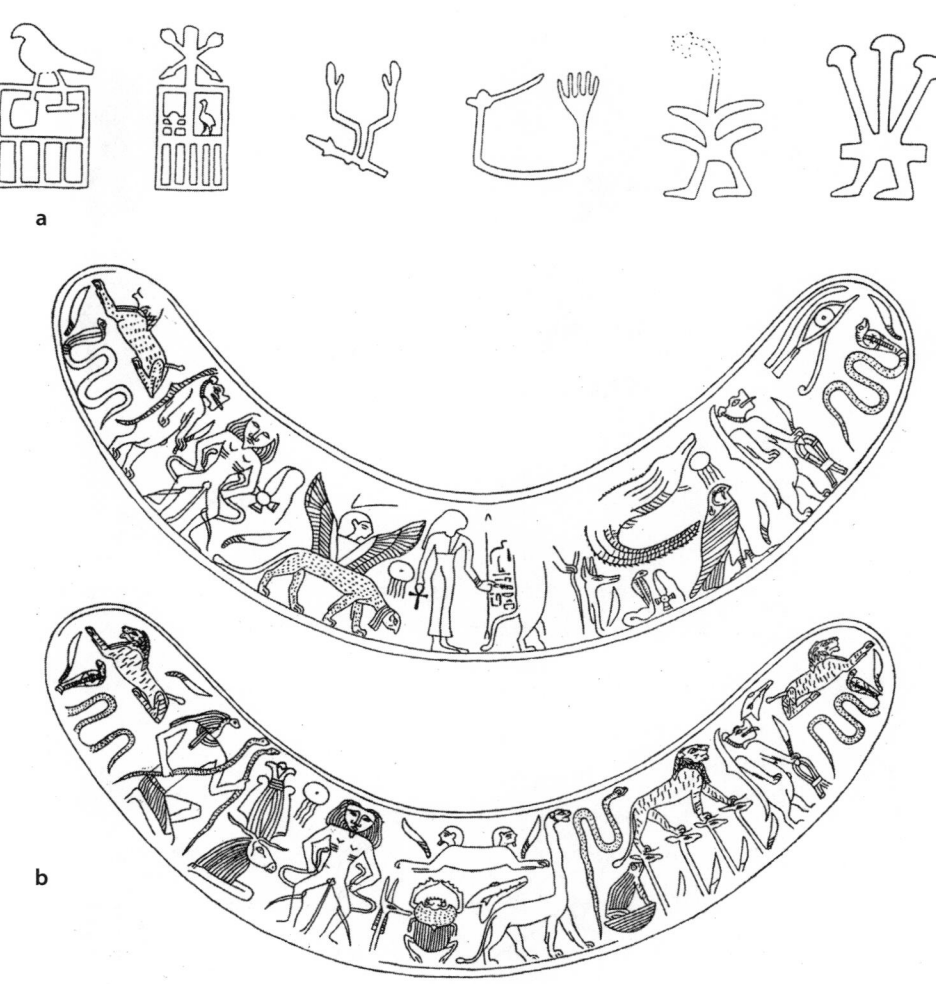

4.3. (a) Composite hieroglyphs of the First and Second Dynasties (ca. 3100–2650 BC; after Fischer 1978); (b) ivory birthing tusk with protective images and inscription, from Thebes, Upper Egypt, ca. 1800 BC (after W.M.F. Petrie. 1927. *Objects of Daily Use*. Cairo: The British School of Archaeology in Egypt, pl. 37: f–g).

formats, and in such diverse products as decorated boxes of wood and ivory,[18] boats made with exotic timber,[19] and perhaps also in the mud-brick echoes of a now-vanished tradition of ceremonial architecture, in which wooden buildings played a central role.[20]

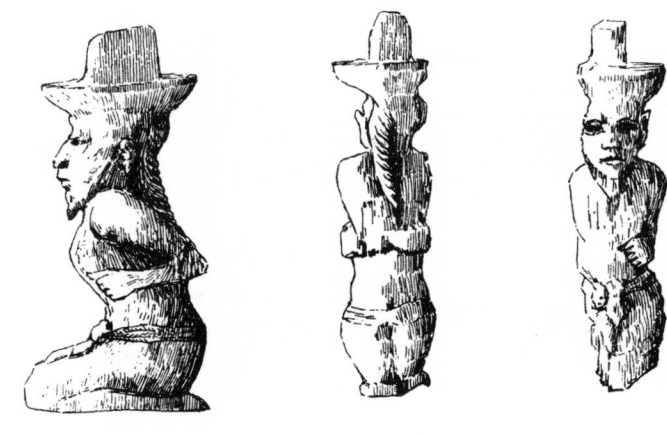

a

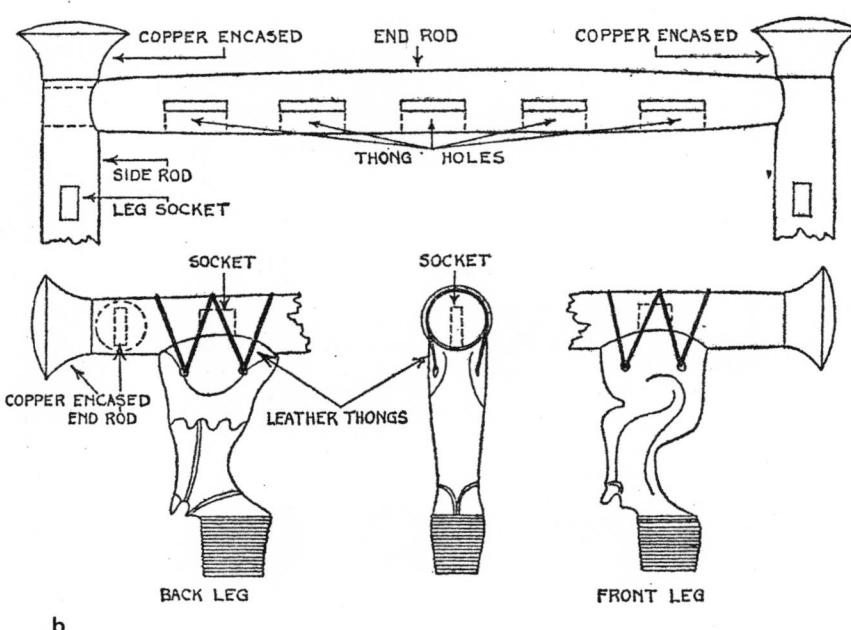

b

4.4. Composite construction in Early Dynastic Egypt: (a) ivory furniture support in the form of a prisoner, with dowel for attachment, from Hierakonpolis, Upper Egypt (after J. E. Quibell and F. W. Green. 1900. *Hierakonpolis I.* London: B. Quaritch, pl. 11: 4–6); (b) construction of a bed frame with bull's leg supports from Saqqara, Lower Egypt, late fourth to early third millennium BC (after Emery 1961, fig. 130; image courtesy of the Egypt Exploration Society).

Mortise-and-tenon joints became a standard method for assembling complex structures out of prefabricated and uniform elements, replacing or supplementing earlier techniques of lashing and binding.[21] In the remains of high-status furniture, which became a focus of craft specialization,[22] these technological changes come together with the world of images depicted on ceremonial objects. Some hundreds of ivory furniture attachments fitted with dowels and slots have been recovered, and can sometimes be identified as three-dimensional versions of figures carved in relief on palettes, knives, and maces, pointing toward the creation of a unified visual environment for elite culture (figure 4.4a).[23]

Like the wooden or ivory bull hooves carved in standard sizes and attached to the legs of carrying beds and chairs (figure 4.4b),[24] images of composite beings slotted neatly into this new material and conceptual world. Their appearance in Egypt—which included the adoption of Mesopotamian prototypes, discussed in the next section—might then appear to have little to do with adaptive "fitness," in the sense of evolved cognitive biases that might favor their reception, and more to do with what Ian Hodder calls a kind of "fittingness."[25] Albeit in a strangely inverted fashion, composites imply within their own structures certain principles of integration that were weakly developed in prehistoric societies, becoming prominent only with the emergence of urban life, and thus helping to account for the flow of images between urban contexts. This is of course a large generalization to make from a single case. In putting it to the test, a broader range of examples is needed.

THE BRONZE AGE: SETTING A SCENE

To set the scene, it is useful to summarize the more commonly recognized features of Bronze Age civilization in the Near East and neighboring regions, those that differentiate it from earlier, Neolithic civilizations. In terms of social structure, the most important are urbanization, the centralization of political and ritual institutions, and the specialization of crafts dealing both in material things and im-material knowledge, including—in some cases—the invention of the earliest known writing systems.[26] These organizational changes were typically preceded by the expansion of commercial networks using new transport technologies (pack animals, wheeled carts, and sailing ships) as well as rationalized forms of commodity production and packaging that accelerated the pace of commerce. They were locally sustained through the intensification of agriculture, using animal trac-tion and irrigation. Only three types of Old World environment could support the combined effects of these processes—albeit at widely varying scales—and all were periodically subject to overexploitation, leading to decline. These were the seasonally refreshed floodplains of major rivers, the rain-fed steppes where farming could be practiced without irrigation, and the more circumscribed valley systems and oases watered mainly by runoff from adjacent highlands.[27]

As Rostovtzeff was already able to perceive, the frequency with which urban life took root in such areas, and its subsequent rhythms of expansion and contraction, were closely related to shifting net-works of trade (figure 4.5). Long-range commerce centered on a restricted range of commodities—notably metals—whose natural distribution lay, not within the centers of population growth, but along their highland interstices.[28] The transformation is first evident during the late fourth millennium BC, on the banks of the Tigris and Euphrates and in the valley and delta of the Nile, where newly formed polities drew in material resources from an extensive hin-terland, reaching from the gold mines of the Nubian Desert to the lapis sources of Afghanistan.[29] In the early centuries of the third mil-lennium, a new frontier of urbanization opened out along the land routes between lowland Mesopotamia and Afghanistan, crossing the copper-rich uplands of the Iranian Plateau.[30]

By 2500 BC, the expansion of maritime trade between Mesopo-tamia and the Indus Valley had stimulated further cycles of urban growth around the fringes of the Persian Gulf,[31] and the process was echoed to the north, on the Syrian steppe, where caravan routes

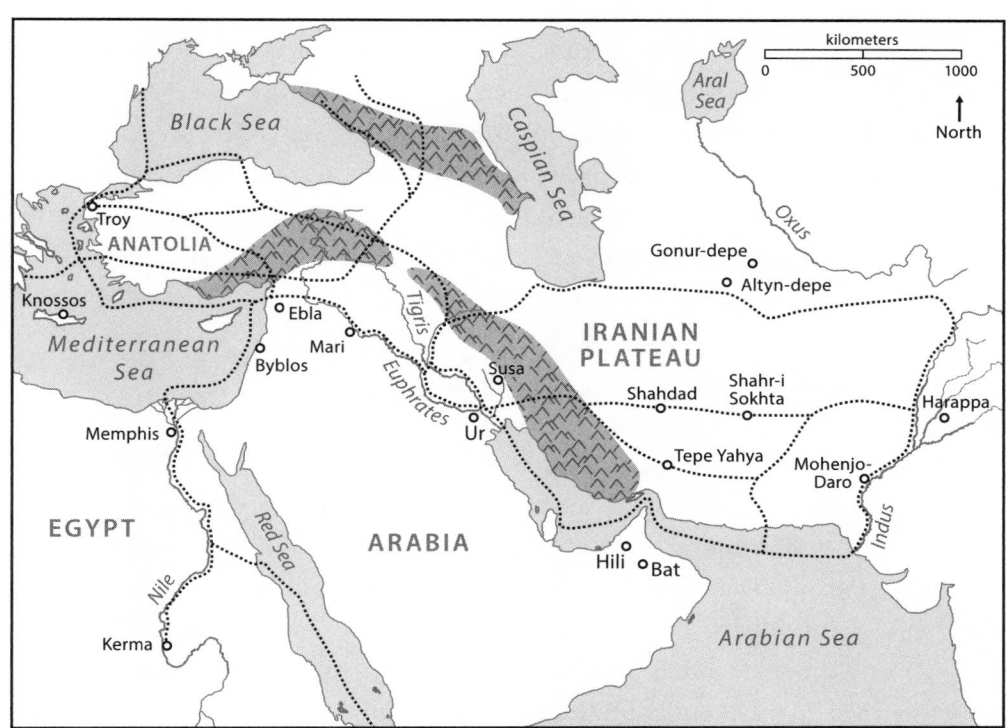

4.5. From the Indus to the Aegean: selected Bronze Age sites and interregional trade routes, ca. 2500–1800 BC.

now converged on the kingdom of Ebla.[32] The cities of the Punjab in turn forged new connections across the Iranian Plateau, extending toward the inland river deltas of Central Asia.[33] There, facing the black sands of the Karakum and Kyzylkum, a distinct form of urban life took root in the final centuries of the third millennium.[34] And at much the same time, a new zone of maritime interaction was opening up along the Eastern Mediterranean seaboard, with momentous consequences for the island of Crete, and its European hinterland.[35]

Each of the areas affected conferred its own cultural foundations upon the basic elements of urban civilization, abandoning certain features of its prehistoric past, but retaining and elaborating others—a role of custodianship usually taken by emergent elites. So, while all share a certain "family resemblance," there are also pronounced differences between them, which arise from their distinct social structures and ecological settings. The differences are clearly evident in styles of urban planning, in settlement forms and patterns, in cosmology and related modes of ceremonial practice, and in the presence or absence of significant institutions, such as literate bureaucracies and sacred kingship.

CIVILIZATION: A MONSTROUS DAWN

It is striking that, in spite of the differences between them, none of the regions I have mentioned adopted the core features of urban civilization without also establishing a visual repertory of fantastic, composite creatures. In some cases, composite animals were initially introduced from neighboring or more distant centers, passing along the same routes of transmission that brought metals, precious stones, and other commodities deployed locally in the legitimization of elite status. An important factor in their dissemination was the use of carved seals to roll or impress complex images onto the clay closures of transport containers, about which there will be more to say in the following chapters.

Such was almost certainly the case with the appearance in protodynastic Egypt of serpent-necked felines and griffins—both of Mesopotamian or western Iranian origin—during the late fourth millennium BC.[36] Upon arrival, these imported composites, which had only recently made their debut on the floodplains of the Tigris and Euphrates, were accorded a central place in the emerging ideology of sacred kingship.[37] On the obverse of the Narmer Palette, an early royal monument, their intertwined necks—now leashed by human keepers in what appears to be a local modification—are ingeniously adapted from the miniature medium of seal carving to form a protective rim around the grinding area, where ritual substances were processed before being ingested or applied to the body (figure 4.6).[38]

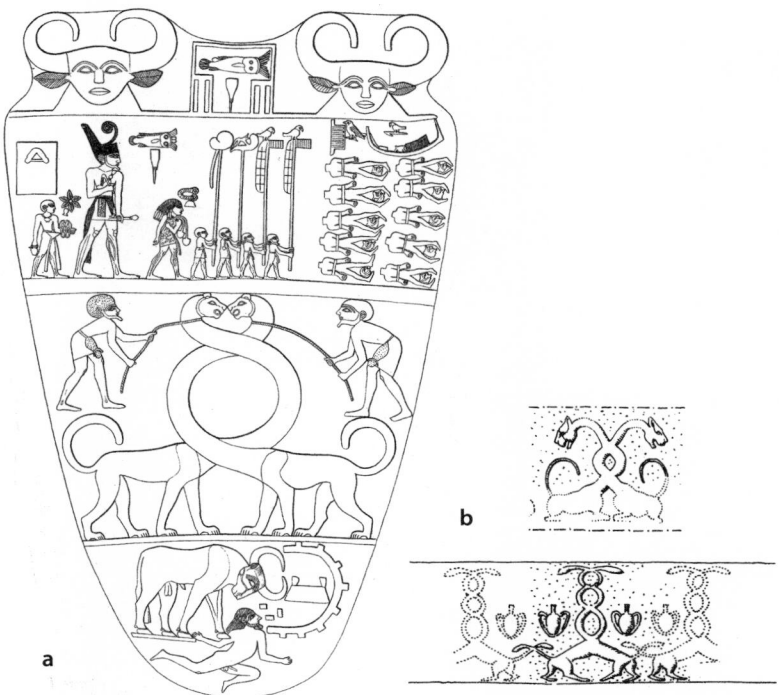

4.6. (a) Serpent-necked felines carved in relief on the central register of the Narmer Palette, from Hierakonpolis, Upper Egypt, and (b) similar figures on cylinder seal impressions from Uruk in southern Mesopotamia, late fourth millennium BC (after Wengrow 2006, figs. 2.1–2.2; Frankfort 1939, pl. 4: d, f).

The composite figure of the goddess *Taweret*, closely associated with the protection of women in childbirth in her area of origin, underwent a similarly impressive transposition.[39] Toward the end of the third millennium (ca. 2300–1900 BC), she leapfrogged from the banks of the Nile to the maritime cities of the Levantine coast, and thence to protopalatial Crete.[40] On arrival, she picked up a mixture of Aegean and perhaps also Anatolian features,[41] paving the way for a series of further monstrous migrations from the east, including the sphinx and griffin, whose watchful eyes overlooked the rebirth of

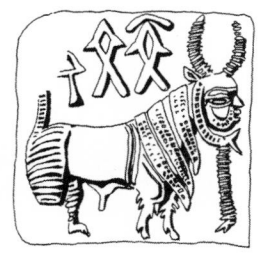 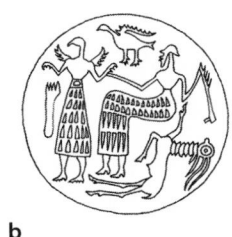 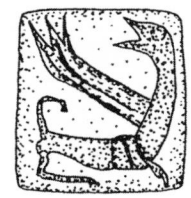

a b c

4.7. Carved intaglio seals from (a) Pakistan (Mohenjo-daro); (b) Bahrain (Karrana); and (c) Turkmenistan (Gonur South), late third to early second millennium BC (after J. P. Joshi and A. Parpola, eds. 1987. *Corpus of Indus Seals and Inscriptions, Volume 1, Collections in India.* Helsinki: Suomalainen Tiedeakatemia, fig. M-302, original photograph by Erja Lahdenperä, courtesy Archaeological Survey of India; K. M. Al-Sindi. 1999. *Dilmun Seals.* Bahrain: Bahrain National Museum, pp. 325–326, no. 249; F. Hiebert. 1994. *Origins of the Bronze Age Oasis Civilization in Central Asia.* Cambridge, MA: American School of Prehistoric Research, Bulletin 42, p. 151, fig. 9.14: 3).

the Minoan palaces in the later Bronze Age (ca. 1700–1400 BC).[42] The same three composites—sphinx, griffin, and *Taweret* in her Minoan form—also traveled farther westward, blending seamlessly into the martial culture of the Greek mainland, and taking up privileged places of residence in the newly constructed palaces at Mycenae, Pylos, and Tiryns (see chapter 6, figure 6.1).[43]

Each of the urban centers that arose earlier in South and Central Asia, during the third millennium BC, cultivated its own brood of composite animals. We do not know their names, but they are clearly recognizable among the regional styles of glyptic imagery produced in the Indus Valley[44] and the Persian Gulf,[45] and subsequently in Bactria and Margiana (figure 4.7).[46] The stone or metal seals on which they were executed were highly durable objects, and occasionally moved over great distances, together with the commodities they marked.[47] The Iranian Plateau and the Syrian steppe have their own, slightly different tales to tell. In the former area, the knitting together of highland and lowland societies into a larger

"Proto-Elamite" culture zone was accompanied by the creation of a new repertory of visual symbols, including wild animals performing human activities such as writing, plowing fields, traveling by boat, fighting with weapons, and bearing offerings (figure 4.8a).[48] As in Mesopotamia, these designs—carried on cylinder seals—were impressed onto the mud closures of commodity vessels, and onto the surfaces of administrative documents and clay door locks, as well as being transposed to larger media.[49] True composites, such as the griffin, also appear in the glyptic art of the Proto-Elamite expansion (figure 4.8b), but overall it was the actions performed by animals— rather than their anatomical forms—that sustained this particular construction of the unreal.[50]

Urban civilization took root on the grassy steppe of inland Syria at the beginning of the fourth millennium BC and intensified toward its end. Southern Mesopotamian influence along the Middle Euphrates is apparent in (among other things) the adoption of cylinder seals bearing images of composites, including types that were transmitted concurrently to Egypt.[51] Around 3100 BC, both Syria and much of northern Mesopotamia witnessed a marked contraction of urban life and long-range commerce. Seals continued in use, and were once again employed in conjunction with painted pottery. Composite animals, however, had no apparent role to play in these more localized forms of cultural display, which spread across the Taurus and Zagros piedmont through social networks comparable in scale to those of Neolithic times.[52] Equally notable is their spectacular reappearance, both in seal imagery and in larger media, during the mid-third millennium BC. Sometimes termed Syria's "second urban revolution," this period saw the reestablishment of long-range commercial ties between the steppe zone and the city-states of the southern Mesopotamian alluvium.[53] Once again, the latter region provided a ready-made repertory of composite figures—now heraldically posed in scenes of combat with human heroes—that was adopted with various modifications by Syrian seal-carvers, and transposed onto more monumental media of display (figure 4.8c).[54]

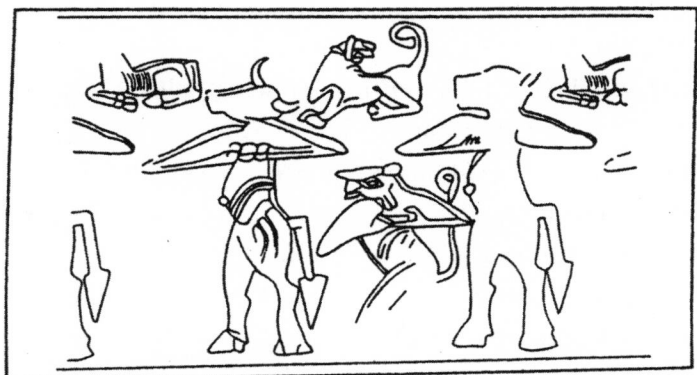

a

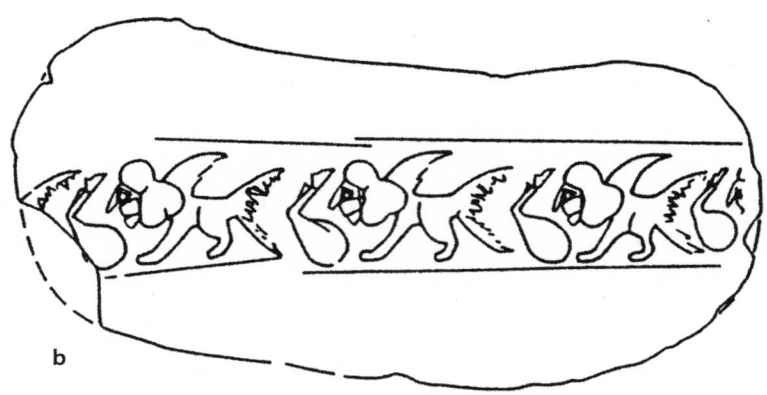

b

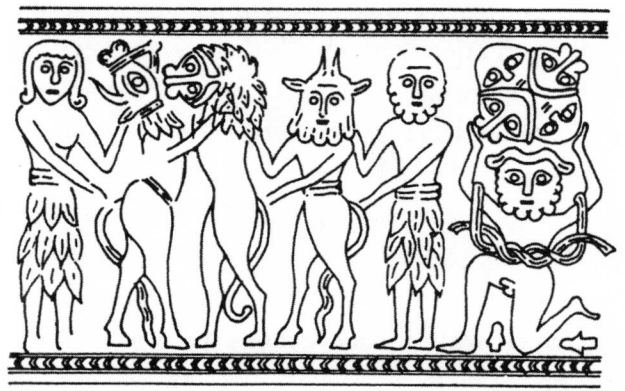

c

A general relationship has emerged between the spread of urban life and the widespread transmission of images depicting composite beings. To an extent, that is perhaps alarming—these distributions are often traceable through just a single, surviving medium: image-bearing seals made of durable materials and their impressions on a variety of malleable surfaces, ranging from the mud stoppers of commodity jars to the strips of clay placed across door-thresholds to deter entry, and—in the cases of Mesopotamia and western Iran—the surfaces of clay documents used to record transactions. Undoubtedly, seals are best regarded as tracers for a wider range of commodities, most of which are not preserved in the archaeological record. Among the latter, dyed and ornamented textiles—the quintessential value-added products of early urban economies—are likely to have played a significant role in the long-range dissemination of visual styles and motifs.[55] In view of these preservation biases, we might be wary of attaching too much significance either to the seals themselves or to the objects they marked. As the earliest known device for mechanically reproducing a complex image, the impact of seal use on the transmission of visual designs nevertheless warrants closer investigation. I will return to this issue in the chapter that follows.

A WORLD DIVIDED: COMPOSITES, COMMODITIES, AND THE URBAN MILIEU

To further define the cultural ecology of the composite animal, I will focus on the initial transition from village to urban life in Mesopotamia. Through their expansive commercial interests, the first cities established along the Tigris and Euphrates rivers provided a stimulus

4.8. (a, b) Cylinder seal impressions from Tall-i Malyan, Fars, southwestern Iran, early third millennium BC (Proto-Elamite; after Pittman 1997: 156, figs. 4c, d), and (c) from Royal Palace G at Ebla, Syria, mid- to late third millennium BC (after Porada 1985: 92, fig. 14).

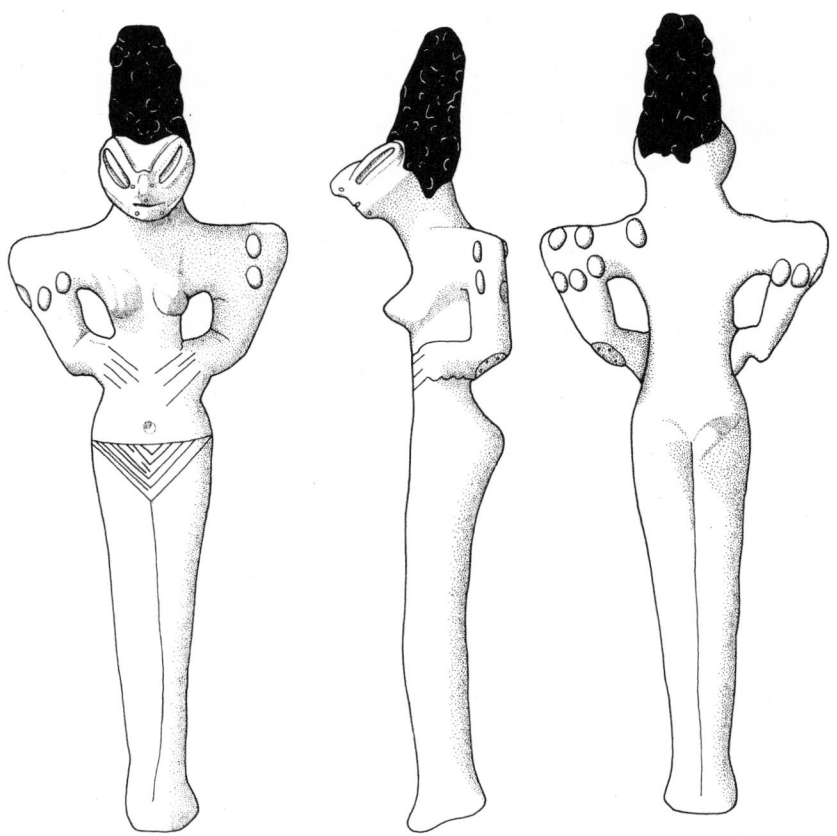

4.9. Composite figurine with female attributes, from a grave at Ur/Tell el-Muqayyar, southern Mesopotamia, fifth millennium BC ('Ubaid period) (after McAdam 2003: 165, fig. 1).

and example for the growth of centers elsewhere. While the institutional foundations of early urban society there remain poorly understood, the Mesopotamian case therefore retains a certain primal status for the wider urban milieu of the western Old World.

Two closely related features of that transition are especially germane to the development of composites: the overall standardization of material culture and the cultivation of new technologies based on modular principles of assembly. The beginnings of these processes lie in small-scale communities scattered across the plains of central and northern Mesopotamia, and in neighboring parts of southern Turkey (ca. 5000–4300 BC). These village societies already display emergent properties of urban life that differentiate them from their Neolithic antecedents.[56] Their ceramic repertories exhibit a new degree of uniformity and an overall reduction of aesthetic investment,[57] and the figurines of this period—which unite elements of human and reptilian form—include complex and relatively standardized forms made by "adding body parts to a central stalk, with features created by carving, painting or application" (figure 4.9).[58]

The use of stone seals to mark the clay closures of commodities was already widely established in Mesopotamia by the fifth millennium BC, but it was only in this phase of village life that their surface designs began to feature an increasingly diverse range of figural images, often depicted with detailed rendering of joints and musculature.[59] The spatial distribution of those images, preserved mainly as impressions on vessel sealings, follows a dense network of highland–lowland trade that extended along the flanks of the Zagros and Taurus mountains, and onto the neighboring plains.[60] In addition to horned animals and humans, creatures with multiple limbs make their first appearance, as does a widely distributed but as yet only loosely standardized image of a human body topped by a goat's head or mask, holding aloft snakes or other dangerous animals (figure 4.10).[61]

With the expansion of urban settlements throughout Mesopotamia during the fourth millennium BC, the trajectory toward standardization and modularity in material culture intensified markedly. Systems of modular construction, based on the assembly of standardized and interchangeable components, are evident not just in imagery at this time, but also across such diverse technological domains as mud-brick architecture and ceramic commodity packaging (figure 4.11).[62] These wider developments in material culture underpinned the invention, around 3300 BC, of the protocuneiform script.[63] This new system of information storage was initially designed for bookkeeping purposes in large urban institutions, which

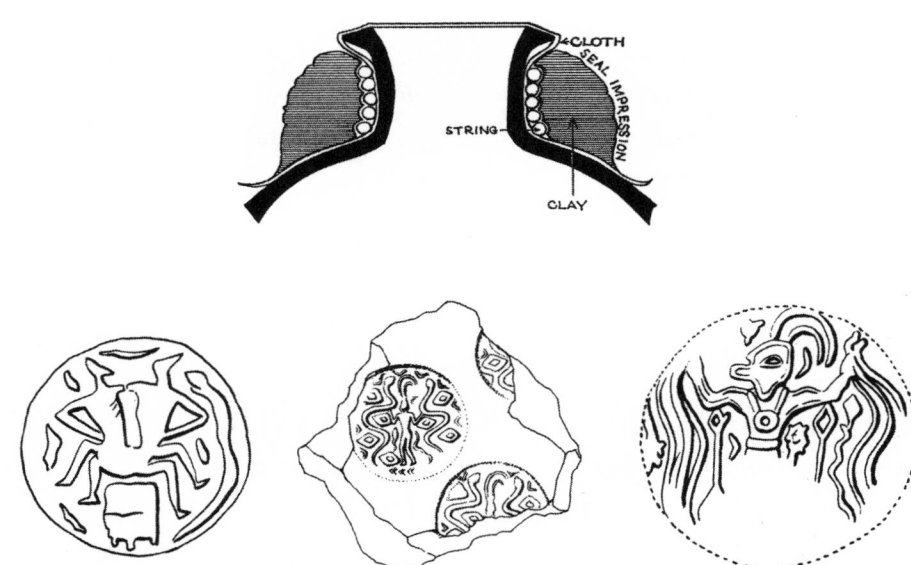

4.10. Illustration of sealing mechanism and examples of images impressed with stamp seals onto the clay sealings of storage vessels, Mesopotamia and western Iran, late fifth to early fourth millennium BC (after Frankfort 1939, p. 2, fig. 1; Amiet 1980, pls. 2, 6, 7).

acted as the religious and economic hubs of the earliest cities. It was based on a principle of differentiation whereby materials, animals, plants, and labor were divided into fixed subclasses and units of measurement, organized according to abstract criteria of number, order, and rank. Many of the earliest known administrative tablets thus functioned in a manner comparable to modern punch cards and balance sheets. In order for such a recording system to function, every named commodity—each beer or oil jar, each dairy vessel, and their contents, and each animal of the herd—had to be interchangeable with, and thus equivalent to, every other of the same administrative class.[64] A smaller number of early inscriptions, known as lexical lists, appear to have had no direct administrative function, and may reflect the intellectual milieu of the earliest scribes, who engaged, as part of their training, in "fanciful paradigmatic name-generating exercises" for a wide range of subjects.[65]

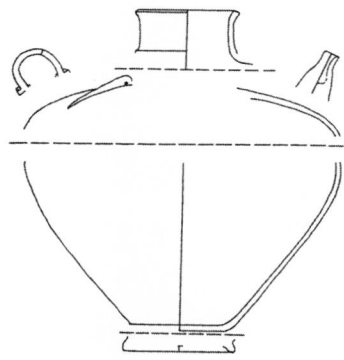

4.11. Pouring vessel showing composite construction, from Habuba Kabira South on the Syrian Euphrates, early urban/Uruk period (late fourth millennium BC) (after D. Sürenhagen. 1978. *Keramikproduktion in Habuba Kabira-Süd*. Berlin: Bruno Hessling, fig. 49).

The invention of a novel repertory of composite figures can be seen to "fit" very logically into this urban and bureaucratic milieu. In pictorial art, new standards of anatomical precision and uniformity, evident in both miniature and monumental formats, echoed wider developments in material culture.[66] Through the medium of sealing practices, miniature depiction remained closely tied to the practice of administration, which required the multiplication of standardized and clearly distinguishable signs for the official marking of commodities and documents. Variability among seal designs was generated through often-tiny adjustments in the appearance or arrangement of figures and motifs. These did not alter the overall visual statement, but allowed each design to fulfill its designated role as a discrete identifier within the larger administrative system to which it belonged.[67]

In its search for new subject matter, it is hardly surprising that the "bureaucratic eye" was increasingly drawn to the possibilities of composite figuration (figure 4.12). Not only did a composite approach to the rendering of organic forms greatly multiply the range of possible subjects for depiction. As Barbara Stafford points out, the counterfactual images that it produced also serve to emphasize details of anatomy that would normally "slip by our attention or be absorbed unthinkingly,"[68] becoming noticeable only when disaggregated from

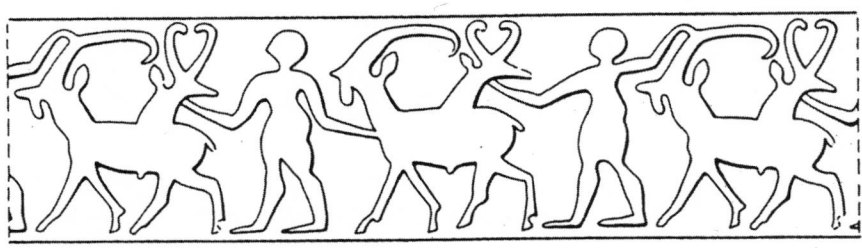

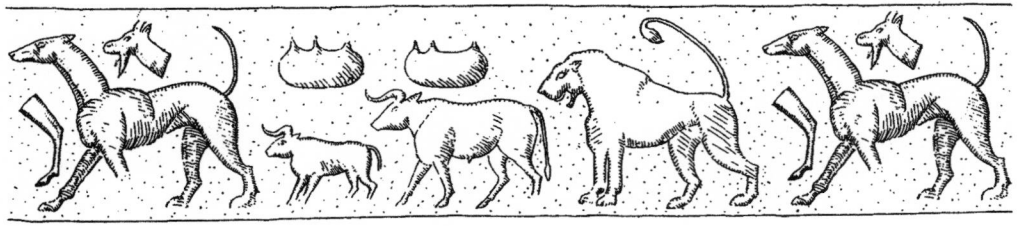

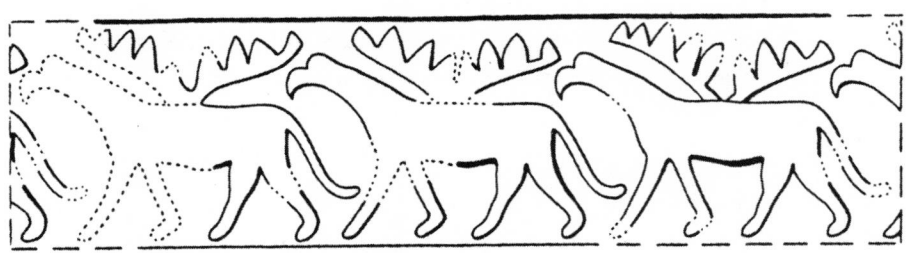

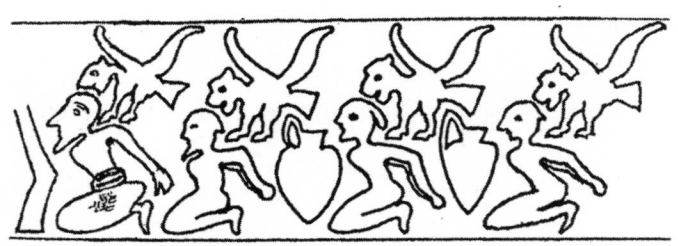

4.12. Cylinder seal impressions showing experiments with composite figuration, from Mesopotamia and western Iran, late fourth millennium BC (after R. M. Boehmer. 1999. *Uruk: früheste Siegelabrollungen*. Mainz am Rhein: Philipp Von Zabern).

their ordinary contexts. Composites thus encapsulated, in striking visual forms, the bureaucratic imperative to confront the world, not as we ordinarily encounter it—made up of unique and sentient totalities—but as an imaginary realm made up of divisible subjects, each comprising a multitude of fissionable, commensurable, and re-combinable parts.

5

COUNTERINTUITIVE IMAGES AND THE MECHANICAL ARTS

> Now the human understanding is infected by the sight
> of what takes place in the mechanical arts, in which the
> alteration of bodies proceeds chiefly by composition or
> separation, and so imagines that something similar goes
> on in the universal nature of things.
> —Francis Bacon, *The New Organon*
> [*Novum Organum* 1620], Works I: 47–69

Imagine that the composite figures I have been describing were not just images of fictitious animals, but actual sentient beings. Their adaptive strategies and evolution could now be described in some detail. We would observe how they have subsisted within a wide range of environments, and that their origins probably extend back as far as our own. But for much of their early prehistory, the relationship of these creatures to humans was largely one of avoidance. They remained generally very rare and special kinds of animals, only occasionally seen, even by those few people who became experts in their patterns of behavior. All of this changed with the emergence of a new and complex type of ecology, around six thousand years ago. Urban and state-like societies offered a setting in which composites could, for the first time, thrive and multiply in significant numbers, leaving a clear and striking taphonomic imprint on the archaeological record.

Clearly not all varieties of composite animal thrived to the same extent, even within their newly discovered niche. Cases of "arrested development" are not difficult to find. One such case may be illustrated by an atypical cuneiform text, known as the Babylonian *Göttertypentext*. Most probably composed in the second millennium BC, it survives only in Neo-Assyrian copies.[1] The text gives a detailed technical program—of just the kind recommended by Leonardo da Vinci (see chapter 2)—for the depiction of composite beings, and uses them in a very unusual way to personify nouns.[2] The following image was intended, for instance, to personify "Grief":

> The head is supplied with a cap and horns of an ox; he is supplied with ears of an ox; the hair hangs loose over his back; the face is that of a woman; his hands are those of a man; he is supplied with wings and his hands are stretched outwards towards his wings; the naked body is that of a woman; his feet stand in the *huppu* posture.[3]

As has often been noted, however, almost none of the composites described in the *Göttertypentext* are attested within the extensive record of Mesopotamian art. Another, and perhaps clearer, case of limited reproduction derives from a palace workshop on Bronze Age Crete. It concerns the miniature creations of the so-called Zakros Master—hyper-composites, combining manifold elements of human and animal bodies—which appear never to have traveled far beyond their point of inception, despite clear attempts to replicate particular images on multiple seals (figure 5.1).[4] If composites, to paraphrase Rudolph Arnheim, "can be bred the cheap or the hard way," then we must also acknowledge that some remained stillborn.

At the other end of the distributional spectrum, we find the contrasting phenomenon of supermobile composites, hopping cultural boundaries with astonishing bravado, and leaving behind them a

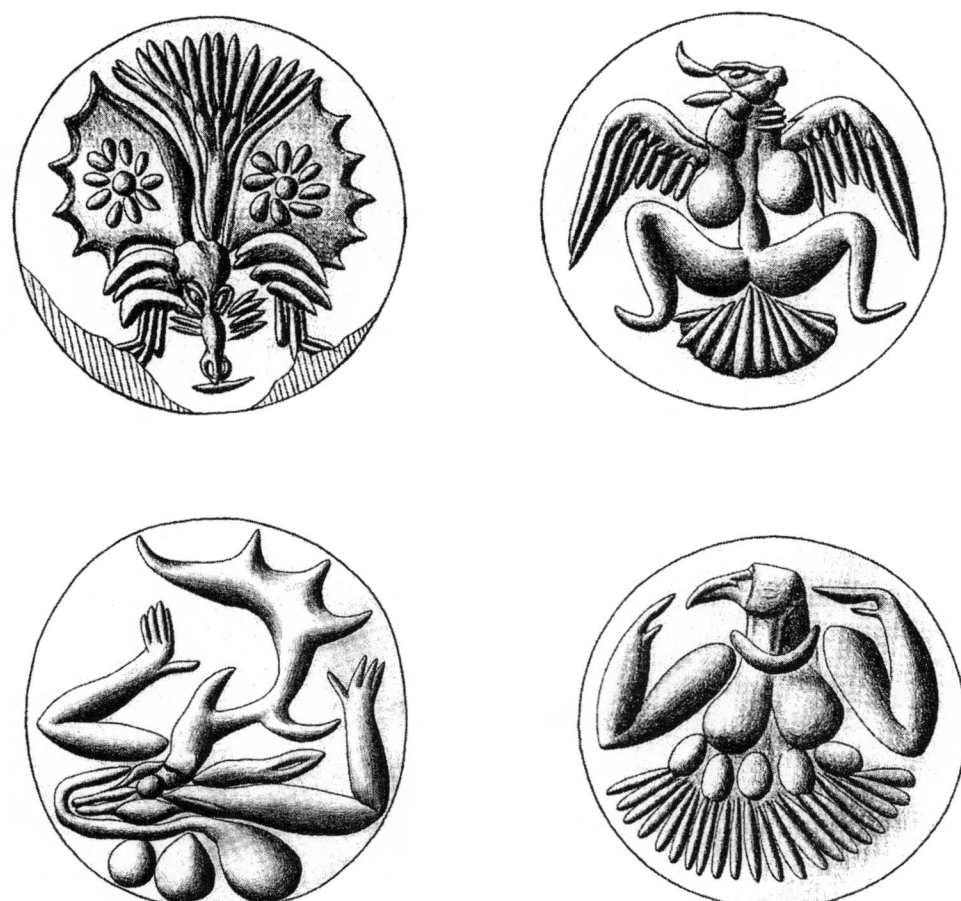

5.1. Hyper-composite figures impressed onto clay sealings, found at the palace town of Zakros on Crete, mid-second millennium BC (after Weingarten 1983, pls. 20–25; courtesy Judith Weingarten).

trail of connections that charts the frontiers of an expanding urban economy. It is unclear how the concept of "fittingness," introduced in the previous chapter, could account for this particular aspect of their distribution. Unlike, for example, the invention of the wheel (another highly contagious feature of Bronze Age culture), the particular form taken by composite figures is unconstrained by technological function. How, then, are we to explain the frequency with which particular composites moved, often in only slightly modified forms, across cultural frontiers? What kind of constraints were acting on their transmission? What was the source of their intercultural stability and appeal?

To address these questions, we need a sharper picture of the processes through which composites spread among different regions. In the following chapter, I will propose some distinct patterns of transmission that are attested across multiple chronological periods and regional settings, shedding further light on the institutional contexts of image transmission in the Bronze and Iron Ages. First, however, more needs to be said about the strange "reproductive habits" of the composite animal, and its strong association with mechanical modes of image making. It may be instructive here to step outside the realm of composites proper and consider another type of image, which occupies a middle-ground between masking and the depiction of imaginary beings: the face of Humbaba, legendary guardian of the Cedar Forest defeated by Gilgamesh in battle, exemplified here by a cast terracotta plaque of the second millennium BC from central Iraq (figure 5.2a). The face of Humbaba and its distant Greek relative the *gorgoneion* exhibit remarkably broad distributions in time and space.[5] Both are to some degree "counter-intuitive" images, in which the "usual conventions and typical classifications [of physiognomy] are syncopated and intermixed." "In disrupting the features that make up a human face," as Jean-Pierre Vernant wrote of the *gorgoneion*, "it produces an effect of disconcerting strangeness that expresses a form of the monstrous, oscillating between two extremes: the horror of the terrifying and the hilarity of the grotesque."[6] Before asserting a relationship between the limited counterintuitiveness of these images and their cultural catchiness, we should consider the technological background to their dissemination. A recent discovery at Tiryns offers a point of departure.

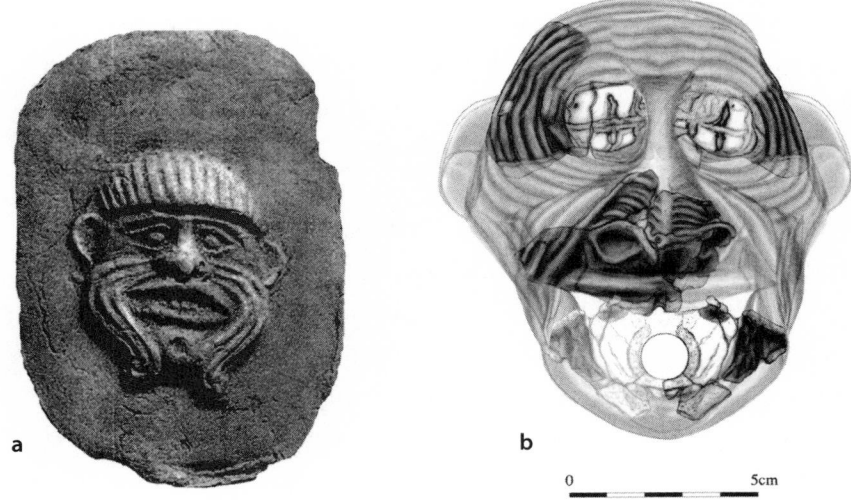

5.2. Furrowed faces on (a) a cast terracotta plaque from central Iraq, early second millennium BC (after M.-T. Barrelet. 1968. *Figurines et reliefs en terre cuite de la Mésopotamie antique*. Volume 1. Paris: Paul Geuthner, fig. 759), and (b) on the reconstructed underside of a mold-made faience cup from Tiryns, Greece, thirteenth century BC (courtesy Joseph Maran and Maria Kostoula).

THE MATERIALITY OF (MINIMALLY) COUNTERINTUITIVE FORMS: A VIEW FROM TIRYNS

There are perhaps few better settings for thinking about the cultural significance of monsters, in the broader colloquial sense, than the ruins of Tiryns, overlooking the Gulf of Argos. The Argolid was Bronze Age Greece's face to the East, just as the Gulf of Corinth—on the other side of an isthmus dominated by the palace at Mycenae—was its face to the West. According to Pausanias, Tiryns became the kingdom of Perseus after his return from the ends of the world with the head of the Gorgon, and his subsequent shaming and exile from Argos.[7] The people of Argos claimed that the lethal prize, which retained the power to kill by its stare, was buried beneath their marketplace: a shrewd insurance policy against future ruination, as well as a potent foundation myth. Pausanias's *Description of Greece* credited the building of Tiryns's walls to another race of monsters, the one-eyed giants, or Cyclopes, who undergo a marked transformation in Greek literature, from Homer's "idle and unruly" troublemakers to the diligent artisans and builders of culture—masters of sculpture and metalworking—that are found in classical sources.[8]

Dating to the thirteenth century BC, the remains of a multimedia workshop are among the recent finds from a destruction layer in the Lower Citadel of Tiryns.[9] The workshop specialized in producing composite faience and sheet metal objects: exotic techniques, imported from the east, and conceivably practiced here by foreign craft-workers. Its products included a distinctive range of head-shaped vessels, the basic forms of which were achieved by pressing successive layers of faience into an intaglio mold. The resulting container was fired to a dark glaze, painted, and ornamented with inlaid eyeballs and perhaps also gold foil attachments. Composite vessels of this kind are rare in Bronze Age Greece, but good parallels are known from urban centers on Cyprus and the Levantine coast, whose trade links to the Argolid are attested in a variety of luxury imports at Tiryns and other Mycenaean palaces.[10]

Having no base, the cups were designed for rapid drinking, probably of wine, in which the act of consumption—from a spectator's point of view—replaced the face of the drinker with that of the creature depicted on the cup. As practical objects, they united the ritual techniques of drinking and masking, both of which imply submission to a public act of metamorphosis. One particular vessel from Tiryns is distinguished by a grotesquely furrowed face, and an unusual aperture in its gaping mouth which could be blocked with a finger while drinking, or used for theatrical effect to emit a gory stream of red liquid, perhaps accompanied by a gargling sound (figure 5.2b). Parallels have been drawn with a contemporary series of terracotta masks that were found on Cyprus, and these in turn echo

Near Eastern depictions of the ogre Humbaba, whose head (bleeding heavily, no doubt, from the mouth) was taken in combat by Gilgamesh, and transformed into a protective image.[11]

Both the faience vessels and the terracotta masks they resemble were most often created by pressing soft material into a reusable mold, which allowed precise replication of a complex—and counterintuitive—version of a face.[12] A late, and apparently isolated, revival of the same technical procedure occurs in the Peloponnese during the Iron Age, when cast gorgonesque masks appear prominently among dedications from the Spartan sanctuary of Artemis Orthia.[13] Its deep origins, however, lie in Mesopotamia, where the one-piece mold was first applied to the reproduction of terracotta images at the end of the third millennium BC and where grotesque faces were produced by this method no later than the beginning of the second, together with a range of composite figures.[14] In considering the popularity of this particular type of image—its ability to become, as Pascal Boyer puts it, "both relatively stable within a group and recurrent among different groups"—we can hardly afford to ignore the material procedures through which it was replicated.

A FURTHER PARADOX IN THE EPIDEMIOLOGY OF CULTURE

From the standpoint of an "epidemiological" approach to culture (see chapter 2), the close association between mechanical techniques of image production and the spread of (minimally) counterintuitive forms is puzzling. It implies a strong element of redundancy—a kind of superfluous cultural prosthesis to cognitive predispositions that are already biased towards the reception of such images. The paradox becomes more acute when we take into account that Mesopotamia, the heartland of composite animals, is also the region where mechanical methods were first widely applied to the reproduction of images, via stamp and cylinder seals, initially, and then also via the terracotta mold (see chapter 4).[15] Moreover, the subsequent proliferation of composites during the Bronze Age follows closely the spread, to neighboring parts of the Old World, of mechanical modes of image production, and of the palace and temple institutions where they were used to promulgate officially sanctioned signs.[16]

Within large-scale social formations (where the origin of commodities was increasingly mysterious and remote), the use of image-bearing seals to mark and secure the containers of goods, taken into the body and household, provided evidence of elite claims to secure the materials of life and wellbeing. For millennia, in the ancient Near East and Mediterranean, sealing devices formed the "canvas" on which an ever-evolving imagery of power and protection unfolded: the comings and goings of gods and goddesses, fabulous animals and kings, intricate scenes of industry and travel, feasting and worship, conquest and defeat—all the dazzling visual innovations of the urban state, harnessed to the most elementary social activity of them all, the sharing and distribution of food and drink. Sealing practices created extended webs of accountability between producers and consumers, while the highly specialized techniques of seal manufacture (using intaglio carving and, from the second millennium BC, wheel-cutting of miniature designs) ensured centralized control over the circulation and modification of designs.[17]

Such practices had a dual effect on the dissemination of images, comparable in some respects to that of the printing press in late medieval and early modern Europe.[18] They provided a method for accelerating the replication of powerful visual formulae, simultaneously restricting their production to a small group of artisans and their elite patrons. This use of mechanical image production to fix ritual values within stable media of transmission, extending their dissemination beyond ephemeral performances into the spaces of everyday transactions, is a distinctive and neglected feature of early state formation in the western Old World. It can be counted among those cultural strategies through which elite groups made "legible" their cosmological and political roles in society,[19] and it has a direct bearing on the distribution of composite figures in the visual record.

Cognition may render us peculiarly susceptible to such images, but viewed in this light their dissemination seems more closely reliant upon technological and political forces.

Might the argument for nurture over nature be pushed further still? Ernst Gombrich, in *The Sense of Order*, appears to suggest just such a possibility, claiming that pictures of imaginary, composite animals—far from being cognitively infectious—confront unusual obstacles to transmission. Of medieval European grotesques he wrote:

> There are no names in our language, no categories in our thought, to come to grips with this elusive dream-imagery in which "all things are mixed." It outrages both our "sense of order" and our search for meaning . . . [those] tendencies which dominate our perception. They alone enable us to form those expectations which can be subsequently confirmed or refuted and which thus permit us to "make sense" of the information we pick up with our eyes. . . . Not only do the limbs of these composite creatures defy our classifications, often we cannot even tell where they begin or end—they are not individuals, because their bodies merge or join. . . . There is nothing to hold on to, nothing fixed, the *deformitas* is hard to "code" and harder still to remember, for everything is in flux.[20]

We are on the verge of a seductive hypothesis, which must be considered if only to be immediately rejected: is mechanical replication in some way a necessary supplement to our innate capacities for recalling and faithfully reproducing counterfactual images on an extended spatial and temporal scale? Let us admit that the idea has its attractions. It provides an economical, if only partial,[21] explanation for the sparseness of composites in the prehistoric visual record, and it tallies reasonably well with their observable spread in later periods. Gombrich, however, offered no evidence—experimental or otherwise—to support the notion that pictures of imaginary creatures might be more difficult to remember and replicate than pictures of living species, and no such evidence has to my knowledge been supplied before or since.[22] Furthermore, any attempt to formulate a causal or universal equation between the use of mechanical reproduction and the dissemination of fantastic imagery confronts an important counterexample, within the ambit of early Old World cultures.[23]

THE CASE OF CHINESE BRONZES

For Mikhail Rostovtzeff, with whom this study began, China marked the end of a journey on the monster's tail, and this chapter will follow suit. An association has long been recognized between the earliest development of cities and urban elites in the valley of the Yellow River and the inception of new modes of display that made great use of fantastic imagery.[24] A by-now-familiar contrast can be drawn, in this respect, with preurban societies in the same region. The Neolithic Yangshao culture (ca. 5000–3000 BC) possessed a rich tradition of painted ceramics, the decoration of which comprises, for the most part, geometric motifs.[25] On those rare occasions when figurative images are present, they depict recognizable animals (such as fish and birds) or schematic human forms.[26] The medium in which imaginary creatures first appear on a significant scale is that of cast bronze vessels (figure 5.3a,b), coinciding with the territorial expansion of Shang power in the latter part of the second millennium BC.[27]

In early China, bronzes were used in the performance of sacrificial offerings, through which descent groups—the basic units of political organization throughout the Bronze Age—sought to maintain favorable relationships with a host of spirit beings.[28] Ceremonial bronze vessels, cast with a sophisticated piece-mold technology, were first produced in quantity with the onset of urban life. They remained central components of dynastic culture for more than a thousand years, spanning the period from around 1500 to 400 BC.[29] Writing before the stylistic development of ritual bronzes had been established,[30] Rostovtzeff proposed a westerly source for the fantastic

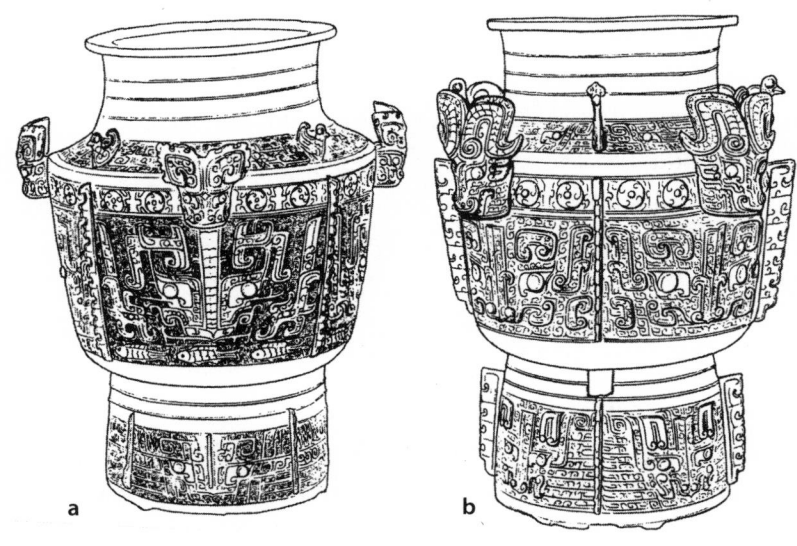

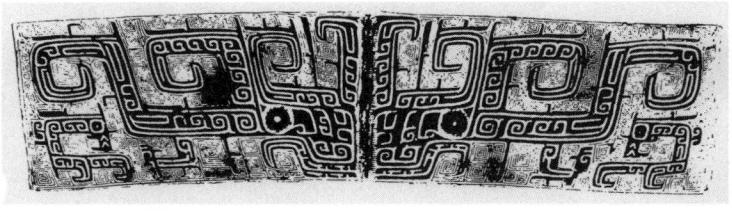

5.3. Bronze vessels from (a) Yueyang, Hunan, and (b) Sanxingdui (Shang period, thirteenth to twelfth century BC, height 50 cm; after drawing by Li Xiating in R. Bagley. 1999. Shang archaeology. In *The Cambridge History of Ancient China: From the Origins of Civilization to 221 B.C.*, ed. M. Loewe and E. L. Shaughnessy, pp. 124–231. Cambridge, UK: Cambridge University Press), and (c) rubbing of *taotie* motif (after Rawson 1987: 27, fig. 9.2).

creatures that appear on Shang and Zhou vessels—in particular, the *taotie* (figure 5.3c), which he confidently referred to as a "Chinese ogre mask"; another design that he called an "eagle-griffin"; and a third that he designated a "dragon." "The main problem of the Chinese animal style," he wrote in 1929, "is to solve the question of the origin of these three fantastic monsters. Is it possible that the same figures, with the same peculiarities, were invented independently both in the Near East and the Far East?." "Have the Mesopotamian fantastic animals and those of China a common origin?'[31]

Chronological impossibilities aside, it has since been suggested that the fantastic creatures of early Chinese art are constructed on quite different principles to their counterparts in the ancient Near East and Mediterranean. Robert Bagley notes a long-standing practice in Chinese art history of viewing prehistoric and Bronze Age images through the retrospective lens of much later, Han-period designs, with their iconic depictions of composite animals.[32] Even the enigmatic carvings on Neolithic jades, popular as grave goods on the east coast of China from the fifth to the third millennia BC, have sometimes been confidently identified as dragon motifs.[33] The dragons of Han art, as Bagley points out, "are not materially different from the ones we see today on placemats in Chinese restaurants." But their remote ancestors, he suggests, "were very different indeed, different in the imaginative processes that produced them and different in their elusive, utterly unfamiliar relationship to animals of the real world."[34]

Accordingly to Bagley, figural designs on Shang and Western Zhou bronzes should be clearly distinguished from the composites of ancient Near Eastern art.[35] The examples of imaginary animals that he considers do not result from clearly articulated variations on animal anatomy. Instead they comprise tantalizing suggestions of organic form that, on closer scrutiny, dissolve back into larger patterns of interlaced lines and projections. In other words, they exemplify just the kind of visual elusiveness that so irritated Gombrich in *The Sense of Order*.[36] Other historians of Chinese art have taken a different approach. Ledderose describes the *taotie* in terms much closer to those I have used for the design of imaginary composites in the western Old World. "The anatomical parts of the *taotie*," he proposes, "may be regarded as modules in a decorative system . . . they are composite, interchangeable parts combined into units." The *taotie*, he suggests, can be constructed from up to ten standard bodily elements (such as body, eyes, nose, horns, and claws), which retain their individual shapes even when detached from the body and left "floating in a sea of spirals."[37]

From a comparative perspective, and within the wider terms of my discussion, what stands out is the systematic avoidance by Chinese bronze casters of mechanical techniques for the replication of complex visual designs, despite the availability of such methods in other media of lower status.[38] Decorative images were painstakingly carved by hand either onto the core from which casting molds were formed[39] or onto individual mold sections.[40] The overall system of manufacture was modular but not mechanical, and reflects the wider principles on which urban crafts were organized:

> For decoration the bronze makers developed a modular system that allowed them to assemble countless combinations from a limited repertoire of motifs and compartments. They also devised a modular technical system for casting their vessels. These systems offered the best solution to the task that the ancient Chinese had set for themselves: to produce high-quality bronzes in sets. . . . To have religious and political life function properly, the Shang aristocracy may have needed in, say, the twelfth century BC, sets of ritual bronzes totaling several thousand units. The bronze makers met the demand by devising modular systems. Modular products lend themselves to a division of labor. They are most smoothly and efficiently fabricated in a production system in which the work is compartmentalized.[41]

Only from around the eighth century BC onward were clay pattern blocks, such as those discovered at the Houma foundry in Shanxi Province, used to impress designs mechanically onto the mold sections from which bronzes were cast.[42] The adoption of this mechanical technique coincides broadly with the absorption, into an existing visual repertory, of restricted elements from a foreign pictorial style that derived ultimately from urban centers of the Near

East.[43] Carried onto the Central Chinese Plain through interaction with nomadic populations, these foreign elements included new ways of constructing composite animals and arranging them in confrontational poses that were formerly absent from Chinese art.[44] In no way, however, can the earlier avoidance of mechanical replication techniques in bronze casting be said to have impeded the dissemination of standard templates for the visualization of imaginary beings, and the overall impact of mechanical reproduction upon this long-established tradition appears to have been quite minimal.

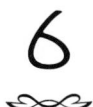

MODES OF IMAGE TRANSFER
TRANSFORMATIVE, INTEGRATIVE, PROTECTIVE

> The interaction of mental images and physical images
> is a field still largely unexplored, one that concerns the
> politics of images no less than the *imaginaire* of a
> given society.
> —Hans Belting, *Image, Medium, Body*, 2005: 304

The distribution of composite figures in the visual record raises a number of intriguing problems for the study of cultural transmission, for which only partial and unsatisfactory solutions have so far been offered. Their impressive transmission across cultural boundaries, to be analyzed further in this chapter, is consistent with the expectations of an "epidemiological" approach to the spread of culture, which would accord them a special kind of cognitive catchiness. But that approach, in its current form, offers no way of explaining why such images become stable and widespread only with the onset of urban life and state formation, beginning little more than six thousand years ago—a mere blink of the eye, on the timescale of biological evolution. In the western Old World, high levels of co-variation occur between figures of this type and mechanical modes of image making, but, for reasons explored in the previous chapter, a direct causal relationship between the two phenomena can be safely ruled out.

More promising avenues of enquiry were opened up in chapter 4. It was argued there that composite figures "fit" within the wider cultural milieu of the earliest cities, where principles of modular construction and reasoning were cultivated for a wide range of activities such as commerce, administration, and display. But this does not explain the recurrence of the same imaginary figures in different cultural settings. In this chapter, I address the latter problem, focusing on the institutional role of externally derived images within centralized (or centralizing) societies. I will suggest that the macro-distribution of composites follows two distinct but regular modes of transmission and reception, to be termed "transformative" and "integrative." The fact that both modes can be exemplified from more than one region and chronological period provides a measure of confidence that the patterns observed, while contingent on particular sets of institutional conditions, are not simply random.[1]

I will then go on to introduce a third mode of transmission, which I term "protective." Attested most clearly in written and pictorial sources of the first millennium BC, it is defined by the magical deployment of images as defense against the spread of illness and misfortune: an epidemiology of representations, yes, but of a more literal kind than envisaged by evolutionary psychology. These three modes do not exhaust the range of processes through which images of composite beings were transmitted among Bronze and Iron Age societies. Closer inspection of written and pictorial evidence from any single region or period would undoubtedly reveal others. Nor are they mutually exclusive. They shade into one another at various points, and the contrasts between them, which often emerge from very different kinds of source material, should not be overstated. I will begin with transformative modes, where the reception of composite figures from an outside source is associated with periods of accelerated structural change in the host society.

TRANSFORMATIVE MODE:
COMPOSITES INTRUDE

Transformative modes of image transfer belong to a wider class of what Andrew Bevan calls "contact phenomena," appearing among communities that were being strongly influenced by external factors, "sometimes attractive, sometimes repellent."[2] Perhaps the most intensely investigated example is that of Iron Age Greece in a period of city-state formation, commercial expansion, and colonization.[3] As Robin Osborne writes of Archaic Greek art:

> The animals of the eighth century are predominantly domestic, those of the seventh century fantastic. Creatures of the imagination colonize pots and dedications alike. Not only do fantastic creatures appear in scenes that show stories, but all sorts of parts of vessels of clay, metal, wood, and stone turn into animals' bodies. From the late eighth century molded snakes writhe their way around the shoulders of Athenian Late Geometric amphorae, and the tripod cauldrons, prestigious dedications at major sanctuaries, sprout griffins' heads.[4]

What Osborne captures so effectively is the intrusion of composites—all of them imported from eastern sources—into the heart of an existing cultural milieu.[5] The wider transformation of that milieu between the seventh and sixth centuries BC has been characterized as one in which architecture changed "from mud-brick huts with reed roofs and rough stone foundations into marble temples with precisely cut blocks and elegant decorative features, sculpture from small, lumpy terracotta figurines into over-life-size statues of marble or bronze, replete with observed detail, and painting from strips of purely linear design into large-scale figure-compositions of considerable refinement.'[6]

James Whitley provides a valuable discussion of local variability in the Greek reception of foreign composites, highlighting their wider social significance at a time of institutional change on the mainland.[7]

He focuses on the dispensation of orientalizing ceramics and metal-work in seventh-century Attica, identifying tensions in the consumption of eastern goods and imagery that were specific to that region, but also shed light on processes taking place in other parts of the Aegean. Throughout much of Greece, the seventh century BC was a period of heightened competition between local elites, whose authority was based on personal ties of loyalty, underpinned by kinship obligations and claims to ancestral status.[8] Since the commencement of the Iron Age, in the tenth century, this aristocratic ideal had been sanctioned through a restricted set of ritual practices, in which the selective display of exotic trade items signaled the attainment of rank and status. Grave goods at that time show a hierarchical pattern of distribution in the archaeological record, and imagery—of chariots, battle scenes, and arrangements of human and animal figures—was carefully rationed on ceramics, metalwork, and ivories. With the exception of centaurs, which first appear on Late Geometric pottery, composites are absent from the decoration of these and other display media.

Whitley considers how, by the late eighth century—in Corinth, Euboea, and other parts of Greece—this established social order was disrupted and transformed through the arrival in increasing quantities of foreign trade goods and through the emergence of a cosmopolitan elite, membership of which was defined and signaled primarily through the use of non-Greek objects, images, and practices. The incorporation into local idioms of display of foreign (mainly Levantine) visual designs, and their percolation across multiple levels of Greek society, is reflected in the increasing popularity of orientalizing motifs—including a variety of composite animals—on painted and incised ceramics, whose decoration emulates the appearance of more prestigious metalwork (see also chapter 1). For local elites, orientalizing objects were both sought after and potentially threatening, an ambivalence that Whitley finds most strongly expressed in the region of Attica, where he detects an attempt to circumscribe the symbolic potential of foreign trade goods within established codes of ceremonial display.[9]

An association between composites, introduced from outside sources, and the reformulation and efflorescence of elite culture can be similarly traced for earlier periods of Mediterranean history. In the centuries directly preceding the emergence of their respective palatial civilizations, both protopalatial Crete (ca. 1950–1700 BC) and Late Helladic I–II Greece (ca. 1600–1350 BC) witnessed an influx of such images carried respectively on Egyptian scarabs and on cylinder seals of the "Common Mitanni Style," and no doubt also on other, less durable media such as textiles and metalwork.[10] In each case, we can follow the incorporation of imported composites into an elite cultural milieu, together with a variety of other exotic practices and commodities. *Taweret* on Crete adopts the role of "libation carrier" and "bearer of offerings," as though she had been born into the rituals of Minoan palace life (figure 6.1a).[11] Likewise, the sphinxes and griffins that arrived on the Greek mainland merged into the newly ordered space of the *megaron*, where sacrifices were performed before the *wanax*, and took up prominent roles in the heroic pageant of Mycenaean kingship (figure 6.1b,c).[12]

Conventional use of the term "orientalizing" to describe such processes is unhelpful. It confines them to a particular spatial and chronological horizon, and to a particular point of view: the Greek or (implicitly) "European" one. It also discourages comparisons with comparable phenomena of cultural fusion and transformation elsewhere. For example, concurrent with her penetration into the Aegean world, *Taweret* also moved south into Africa, where she was adopted by indigenous elites whose emergent centers of power lay astride the Third Cataract of the Nile, at Kerma.[13] There her protective figure appears at the heart of royal rituals, arrayed along the head and foot supports of ceremonial beds—traditional carrying equipment for deceased members of the court en route to their monumental tombs, where both human kin and cattle were sacrificed in spectacular burial rites.[14]

Further comparisons can be drawn with the much earlier reception of Near Eastern composites in protodynastic Egypt, at the end of the

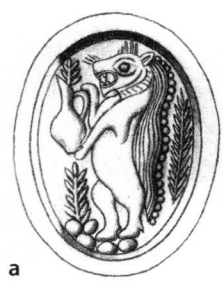
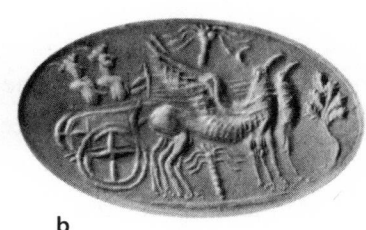

a   b

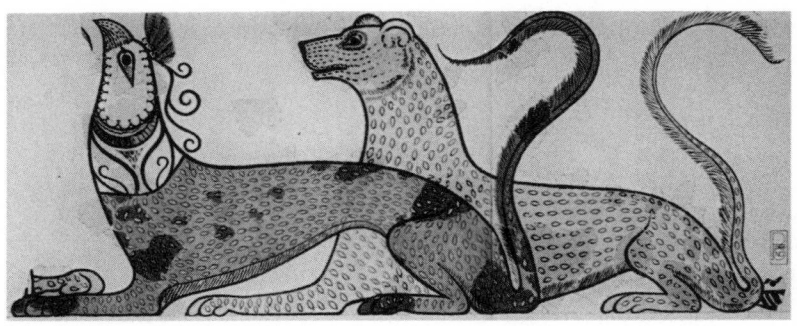

c

6.1. (a) Cretan rendering of *Taweret* on a stamp seal impression from Phaistos; (b) griffins pulling a chariot on an impression of a gold signet ring from a *tholos* tomb at Anthia in Messenia, Greece, mid-second millennium BC; and (c) griffin-lion pair on a wall frieze reconstructed from fragments found in the later palace at Pylos, thirteenth century BC (after Weingarten 1991, p. 22, fig. 3; Krzyszkowska 2005, p. 252, fig. 486, photograph of impression by Olga Krzyszkowska; M. Lang. 1969. *The Palace of Nestor at Pylos in Western Messenia II: The Frescoes*. Princeton, NJ: University of Cincinnati and Princeton University Press, pl. P-21C46, courtesy of the Department of Classics, University of Cincinnati).

fourth millennium BC, similarly associated with an efflorescence of elite culture and with the coalescence of new institutions—in this case, the unification of the "Two Lands" of Upper and Lower Egypt under a form of sacred kingship that lasted, in its essentials, until the Greco-Roman period. The core ingredients, discussed in chapter 4, are all there, unfolding over a similar time span of three to four centuries: an influx of composite figures from distant sources, carried on expanding routes of long-distance maritime and overland trade; their incorporation into culturally salient objects and practices that were previously free of them; and their deployment by new and powerful groups whose influence transcended that of earlier factions on both the local and supra-local levels.[15]

I have defined a recurrent mode of cultural transformation, with recognizable archaeological traces and consistent manifestations across multiple regions and periods. As first exemplified in the fourth millennium BC, the pattern is one of disruption and accelerated change—characteristic of the periods labeled "proto-" or "archaic"—in which received cultural categories are brought into question through heightened exposure to foreign influence. The incorporation of composites, originating outside the established boundaries of a given cultural milieu, is a consistent feature of these transformations, from protodynastic Egypt to Archaic Greece. In no instance can any simple causal relationship be posited between institutional change and the adoption of a foreign bestiary in art or ritual. It is notable, however, that in each of the cases described, exotic composites are associated with the material culture of social elites in the process of self-fashioning, and were accorded discursive prominence through their incorporation into important rituals and ceremonies. The cumulative unfolding of this cultural pattern across an ever-widening area created a common fund of fantastic imagery, shared by Bronze Age elites from the Near East to the Aegean. The growth of this common reservoir of images, connecting elite worlds via the otherworldly, was a precondition for my second mode of cultural transmission: the "integrative" mode.

INTEGRATIVE MODE: COMPOSITES MOVE BETWEEN

The transmission of images in the integrative mode corresponds closely to the development of what are often termed "intercultural" or (anachronistically) "international" styles in the art of the ancient Near East and Mediterranean—that is, elite visual styles blending elements of diverse cultural origin, and resisting identification with particular craft centers or "schools."[16] Marian Feldman, in her book *Diplomacy by Design*, has done much to clarify the distinctive features of inter-cultural style objects in the later Bronze Age, including the pervasive presence not only of imaginary animals (notably sphinxes and grif-fins) but also of composite, fantastical plants among their surface dec-oration. During the fourteenth and thirteenth centuries BC, luxury goods took on common forms across cultural boundaries, working to consolidate otherwise fragile commercial and political bonds through their circulation as gifts and countergifts. At this time of intense inter-regional diplomacy between the royal courts of the Eastern Mediterra-nean, imaginary landscapes—ornamenting the highly crafted surfaces of luxury furniture, vessels, and vehicles—reveal, in their distribution, the cosmopolitan face of courtly life—the desire for mutual recogni-tion and integration across often tense cultural boundaries, negoti-ated amid the ever-present uncertainty of dynastic politics.

International correspondence of the period, preserved mainly from cuneiform archives found in New Kingdom Egypt and Hit-tite Anatolia, reveals a sharp competitive edge to royal exchange, and indicates the risks of diplomatic failure entailed by inadequate or inappropriate gestures.[17] It is within this ostentatious and fissile world that Feldman locates the decoration of "international style" objects. Composite animals typically feature there in scenes of pre-dation where they are incorporated, either as violent opponents or protective allies, with images of real wild animals such as lions (fig-ure 6.2).[18] She suggests that both composite creatures and imaginary plants (notably the "stylized voluted palmette") serve to locate this imagery "outside the realm of the physical world and into 'otherness' that could be either threatening or protective."[19] The evidence as-sembled by Feldman is extremely diverse, and the characteristics of the integrative mode may be easier to define if we consider an earlier example, more tightly focused upon a single medium.

During the middle and later part of the third millennium BC, in the Early Bronze Age, highly ornamented vessels made from a

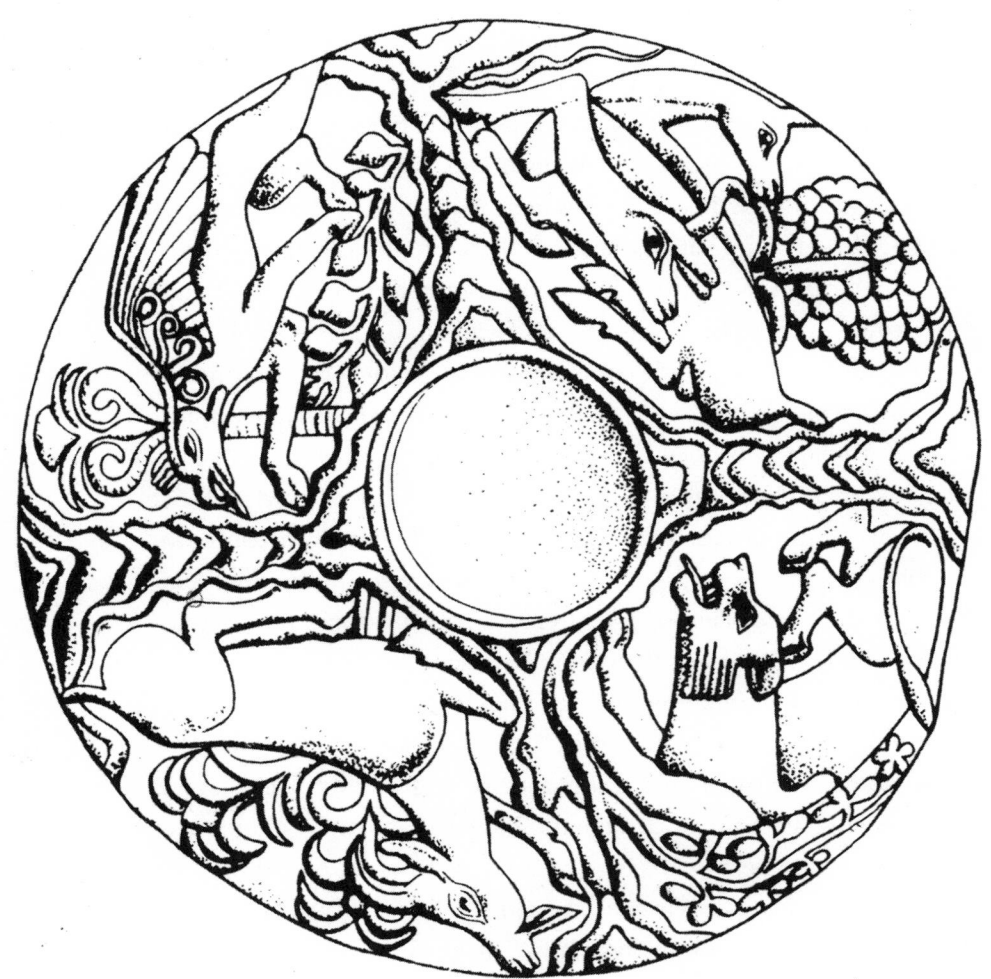

6.2. Wooden box lid with relief carving of a landscape populated by real and imaginary animals, found at Saqqara in northern Egypt, ca. 1400 BC (after Morgan 1988: 52, fig. 41).

soft, dark stone known as chlorite achieved an extremely wide distribution, reaching from Central Asia to the Euphrates, and passing across a multiplicity of cultural and political boundaries.[20] Such vessels are most frequently documented between the central and southern coastlines of the Persian Gulf and the city-states of lowland Mesopotamia and Khuzistan, where they have been found in temples

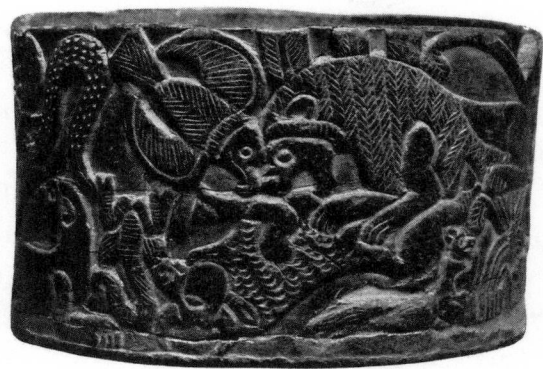

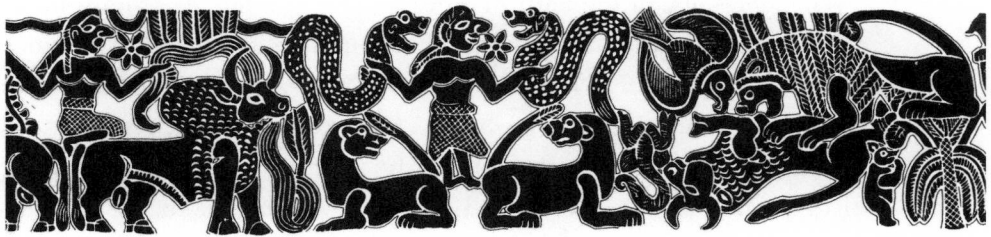

6.3. Soft-stone vessel with intercultural-style ornament from Khafaje, Iraq, mid-third millennium BC, and rolled-out reproduction of its surface decoration (after H. Frankfort. 1954. *The Art and Architecture of the Ancient Orient*. Harmondsworth: Penguin, p. 19, fig. 9. © The Trustees of the British Museum).

dedicated to various deities. Carved with metal tools, these "intercultural style" containers, as they are known, were highly individualized both in form and decoration.[21] Each was densely ornamented from lip to base on its outer surface with varying combinations of patterned relief carving, figural attachments, and inlays of colored stone and shell (figure 6.3). Composite animals figure prominently, most often in the form of lion-headed serpents, but also including standing bull-men.[22] They are among those images of living beings whose bodies are animated by paint and colored inlay. Scorpion-men and lion-men, sometimes shown in the "master-of-animals" pose, are known on chlorite vessels recovered in southern Iran, but as yet these have no clear parallels from excavated contexts.[23]

Sources of chlorite were concentrated in central Arabia and around the highland margins of the Gulf of Oman, and production centers for intercultural-style vessels have been identified at Tepe Yahya and perhaps also at Konar Sandal, in the vicinity of Jiroft.[24] The location of these sites in the Halil River basin, with ready access to a major maritime outlet at Bandar Abbas, suggests a commercial orientation for the development of intercultural-style ornament, as noted long ago by Philip Kohl.[25] This is borne out by its characteristic range of figural designs, which borrow skillfully from neighboring traditions of glyptic art, blending landscape elements—including natural types of flora and fauna—from sources as distant as the Indus Valley and Mesopotamia. The choice of chlorite as a decorative medium is also significant in this context. Its absorbent and insulating qualities were technologically suited to a range of cultic activities, such as the burning of unguents and the preparation of cosmetics and perfumes—objects, and composites, for all manner of special occasions.[26]

Vessels of this kind would have fitted especially well into a prestigious suite of commercial packages that included tree resins and oils traded northward from the Arabian side of the Gulf, where a further production center is likely to have existed on Tarut Island, in the area referred to by Mesopotamian sources as *Dilmun*.[27] Their easily worked surfaces also invited secondary markings, as with a jar from the Inanna Temple at Nippur, to which a dedicatory inscription has been added.[28] Another widely employed decorative motif was the paneled façade, associated with temple structures and ritual offerings in Mesopotamia since the late fourth millennium BC. It often appears surrounded by swirling motifs, perhaps evoking billowing fumes, and suggesting a possible function for these vessels as containers for incense or other substances burned for their fragrance and cleansing effects.

On intercultural-style vessels of the Early Bronze Age, as on international-style objects of the later Bronze Age, composite animals are rarely accorded the kind of discursive prominence that they achieved in transformative modes of transmission. Within the integrative mode, they are usually incorporated into vibrant pictorial landscapes, interacting on an equal footing with real animals as predators or protectors—a more muted visual status, in keeping with the sensitive decorum of interelite exchange. Having defined the essential features of transformative and integrative modes, a third mode of image transfer can now be identified. It is attested through an unusually rich body of evidence from Mesopotamia, casting light on the mobilization of composite animals as vehicles of protective magic, directed against the spread of disease and misfortune.

PROTECTIVE MODE: COMPOSITES DEFEND BOUNDARIES AND THRESHOLDS

To the Neo-Assyrian period in Mesopotamia, corresponding to the first half of the first millennium BC, belong cuneiform documents containing detailed instructions for the manufacture and use of composites.[29] Texts of this kind have been found in the royal tablet library of Nineveh, in the House of the Exorcist at Assur, and at other urban locations. As Frans Wiggermann puts it, they prescribe "rituals for the defense of the house against epidemic diseases, represented as an army of protective intruders."[30] The rituals comprise a series of technical acts, some perhaps more symbolic than real,[31] which resulted in the production of a small militia of composite figures, accompanied by images of armed deities and guard dogs. The texts also contain detailed instructions for the strategic placement of these miniature figures within and around the designated building, as a first line of defense against invisible and malevolent forces; among the equipment they carry are canonical instruments of cleansing and purification, such as the bucket and censing cone.[32]

The importance of these written sources, as Wiggermann and others have pointed out, extends beyond their local contexts of storage and use. They offer direct insight into the creation and purpose of an important class of composite figures at a time when Assyrian cultural and political influence extended from the orientalizing world of the Eastern Mediterranean to the highland kingdoms of the Caucasus and western Iran.[33] Moreover, the images that are their main concern can be matched with some certainty to those depicted on contemporaneous terracotta plaques and figurines, excavated from the foundations of public and private buildings (figure 6.4).[34] In some cases, the descriptions of these miniature composites also accord well with the appearance of monumental figures: protective spirits that guarded the sculpted palaces of the Neo-Assyrian kings;[35] and some—such as the "Scorpion-Man" and "Bull-Man'—have regional genealogies extending back to the third millennium BC.[36] Wooden images of protective spirits are also mentioned in the texts, but have not survived for inspection.[37]

Like the demons they were intended to repel, the powers of those supernatural agents invoked in the ritual texts were ambivalent. The purpose of the rituals, and of the technical process of forming a miniature figure, was to obtain a degree of control over them, harnessing them to the domestic realm as a kind of spiritual fortification against outside threats and pollution. The texts make it clear that this could be achieved only with the aid of the gods, which was called upon through the observance of cleansing and sacrificial rites during the making of effigies, and by the consecration of their wood and clay with purifying materials: gold and silver tools for the (symbolic) cutting of wood, and precious stones such as carnelian, to be cast into the pit from which clay was extracted.[38] The choice of materials is never explained, but it seems significant that all originate in distant highlands beyond the familiar world of cities, extending the spatial logic of an official worldview in which mountains constituted not just the margins of a civilized, lowland world but also its ontological opposite.[39] Geographical remoteness is also directly evoked in inscriptions that empower protective spirits to send the demons "3,600 miles" away from their intended human targets, and also in

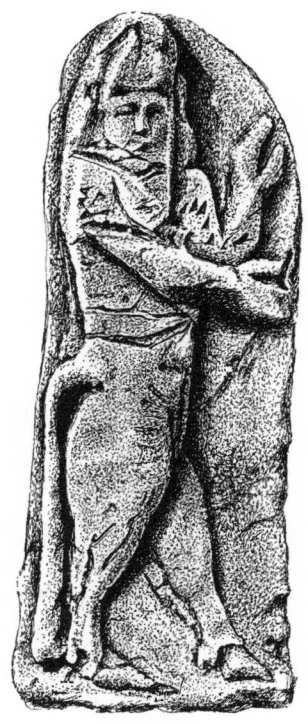 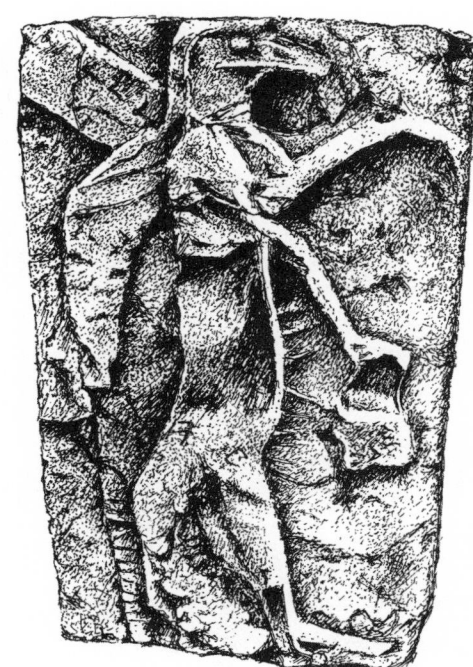

6.4. Mold-made terracotta plaques (heights ca. 12 and 14 cm) with images of protective spirits, from Assur in northern Iraq, early first millennium BC (after Rittig 1977, figs. 22, 40).

the depiction of harmful demons—such as the child-devouring *La-mashtu*—as equipped for long-distance travel over land and sea (figure 6.5).[40]

Some more general observations can be made about these documents, and the associated corpus of images. The first concerns the highly structured, ritualized, and restricted genre of image production to which they belong. Neo-Assyrian composites came in standard sets and assemblages, and the rituals gave precise instructions as to their appearance and proper locations around the house. Every detail of manufacture was clearly set down: the various components

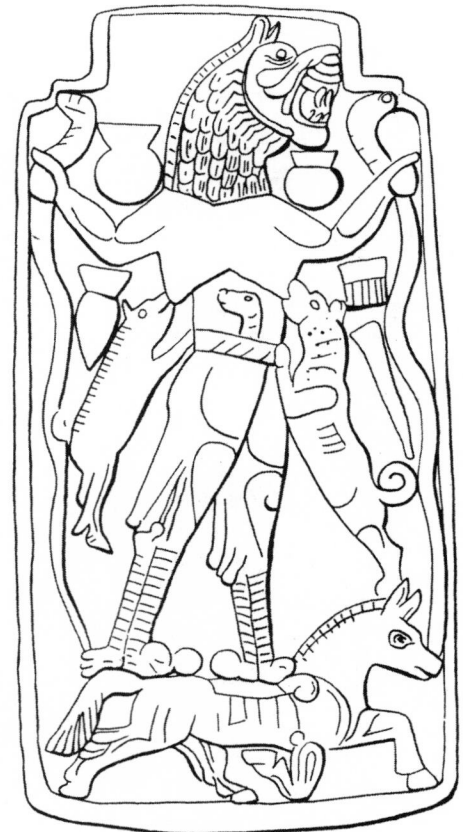

6.5. Stone amulet with image of *Lamashtu* standing on a donkey (probably early first millennium BC, acquired by Leonard Woolley and sometimes attributed to Carchemish, on the Syria-Turkish border; its provenance is in fact unclear; after Burkert 1992: 84, fig. 5).

of the body (including model wings, horns, and incised scales); its outer treatment with colored pastes; the written incantations to be inscribed on its surface; the weapons and instruments of purification that it was to carry; to which hand each should be attached; and in what order all these acts were to be carried out.[41] The counterfactual properties of the resulting image were thereby constructed through a whole series of explicit ritual and technological procedures extraneous to its cultural form—procedures we would be quite unaware of, were it not for the survival of relevant written sources.

Making a magically effective composite was then no ordinary technical act, but one guided by strict and preordained regulations, requiring access to special (and often exotic) ingredients and skills, including literacy. While the miniature clay composites of the Neo-Assyrian period may appear, on first inspection, to belong to the same general class of "popular" imagery as prehistoric figurines, their conditions of production are therefore worlds apart. Behind each composite form lurks the complex cultural apparatus of the imperial state, with its carefully administered and ever-expanding archives of occult knowledge, its stores of exotic and magical materials, and its concentration of ritual, medical, and technological expertise.[42] Edith Porada perceptively observed that this centralized management of the spirit domain is surely less a proof of "terrible superstition" than of "trust in the exorcists, the 'men of science' of the day who had libraries of protective rituals at their disposal."[43]

The ability of rulers to concentrate such skills and resources within the imperial center rendered its peripheries—to which terrifying demons such as *Lamashtu* did indeed travel—peculiarly vulnerable, in a way that goes beyond political or economic insecurity, threatening the psychological foundations of social life.[44] It is this particular construction of the alien, composite image that may in some (but clearly not all) cases forge a link with the "transformative mode" of transmission, as defined earlier in this chapter. In his analysis of the Perseus-Gorgon myth, David Napier describes one such process, played out on the margins of Neo-Assyrian imperial and commercial influence.[45] Imported composites, he suggests, were given discursive prominence in archaic Greek art as points of engagement with the foreign; as a means of encompassing and modulating the transformative effects of exposure to outside influence, in a way that served the interests of particular groups in local arenas of status competition. The face of Gorgon—prominently mounted on architectural thresholds[46] and displayed on the surfaces of feasting equipment—was interlaced with characteristic forms and postures of alien composites, appearing variously on the hybrid body of a centaur or in the "mistress of animals" pose familiar from the protective imagery of the Near East. Visual experiments of this kind, according to Napier, were a matter "of attaching through iconography, and of legitimizing through mythology, images and relationships that in themselves are forceful," reflecting the "Greek desire to have their own Gorgon be equal to or superior in power to these demons of the Near East, to compete and win out, if you will, on similar iconographic terrain."[47]

COMPOSITES AS CAPITAL AND AS INTELLECTUAL PROPERTY

In exploring some of these more elaborate modes of image transfer, the more obvious entanglements of composites with the circulation of luxury goods and materials should not be overlooked. Quantities

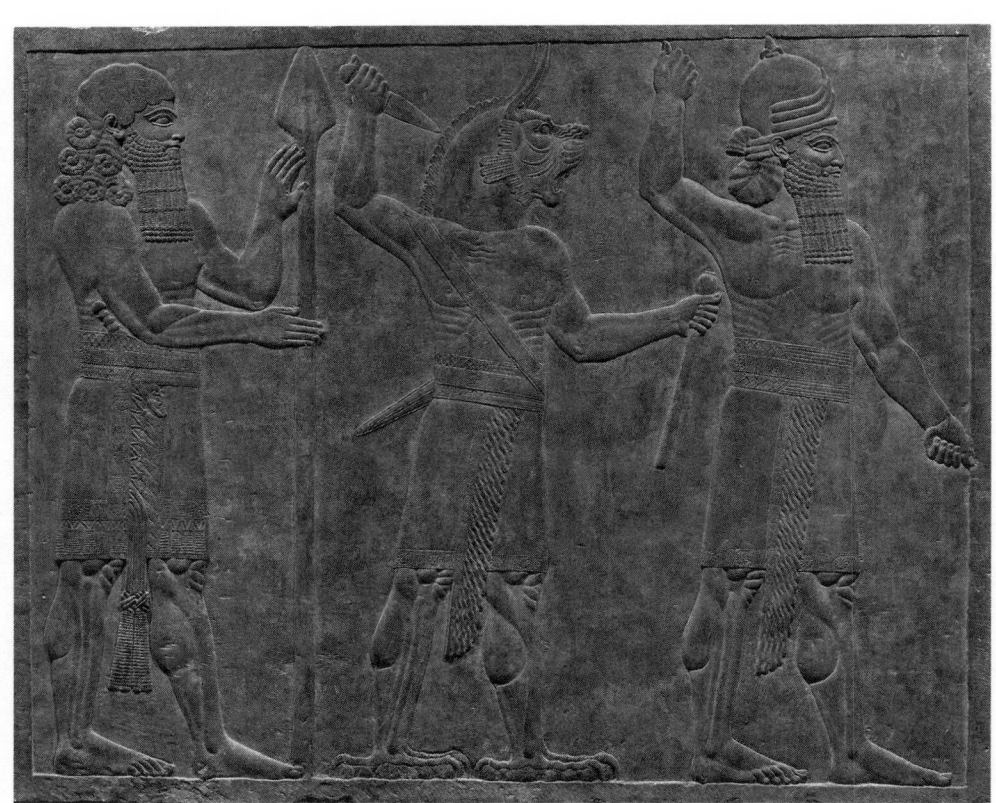

a

of expropriated Phoenician and North Syrian ivories, recovered from Assyrian palaces of the early first millennium BC, are just one indicator of the scale on which ornamented materials, also including decorated textiles and metalwork, moved as a consequence of political and military expansion.[48] Prestige metalwork in particular, by virtue of its recyclable nature, carried intrinsic commodity value regardless of its decorative content.

Coerced movements of precious objects could also stimulate more complex processes of cultural appropriation. Mehmet-Ali Ataç provides an example in his analysis of the relationship between Ninevite palace relief and Egyptian funerary art (figure 6.6), viewed against the backdrop of Assyria's conquests on the Nile in the seventh

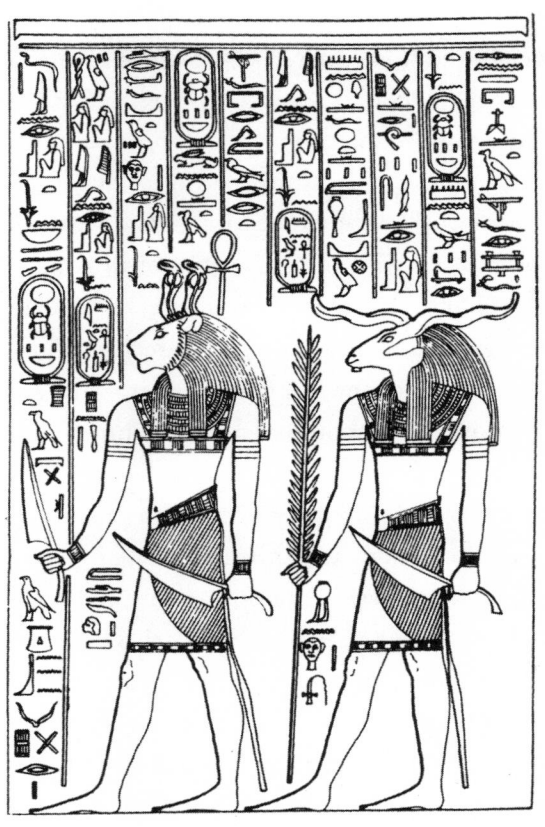

b

6.6. Protective spirits from two worlds: (a) monumental relief carving of an *ugallu* from the North Palace at Nineveh, Iraq, ca. 640 BC (© The Trustees of the British Museum); (b) guardian figures on a funerary shrine of Tutankhamun, Eighteenth Dynasty of Egypt, fourteenth century BC (after E. Hornung. 1990. *Valley of the Kings. Horizon of Eternity*. New York: Timken, p. 73).

century BC.[49] The taking of Thebes, in Upper Egypt, made available to the Ninevite court not only the imperial monuments of the New Kingdom, by then some centuries old, but also the human resources of the Egyptian palaces and temples. Among the movable assets taken to Assyria were scribes and ritual specialists, bringing with them exotic techniques of healing, protective magic, and the interpretation of dreams.[50] Three millennia after their first migration from Mesopotamia to the Nile, images of composite beings—and associated forms of specialist, occult knowledge—may therefore have traveled back in the opposite direction as trophies of war.

SECURING BOUNDARIES IN A FRAGILE WORLD

At what is admittedly a high level of generality, the modes of image transfer defined in this chapter can be seen to share an underlying problematic. Each is associated to some degree with environments of heightened risk and uncertainty, where failure to properly negotiate boundaries can lead to catastrophic consequences. Within the transformative mode, status accrues to those groups within society who can establish stable relations with an encroaching outside world. The integrative mode is associated with the tense theater of courtly diplomacy, with its fragile alliances and fateful transgressions. And the protective mode, shading into the other two, is a direct response to threats against household and person, in which preemptive ritual attacks are launched upon the demonic carriers of illness and misfortune.

Against this backdrop, the cultural ecology of the composite figure comes into clearer focus. It can now be defined not only in terms of morphology—that is, the "fit" between composites and the technological milieu of the first cities (see chapter 4)—but also in terms of institutional dynamics. Time and again, these otherworldly anatomies provided the locus for a heightened cultural interplay between "self" and "nonself," condensing some anticipated danger into an image that could be fixed and managed within existing structures of meaning. The cosmos occupied by composites was a fragile and fissile one, presided over by the threat of uncontrolled transformations, and confronted by the prospect of immanent corruption, marginalization, or disintegration. If we are seeking a biological analogy for their properties of transmission, then we might best look not to the field of epidemiology but to that of immunology, which centers on the procedures available to the body (and, by extension, to the body politic) for discerning and neutralizing outside threats.[51]

CONCLUSION

PERSISTENT, BUT NOT PRIMORDIAL:
EMERGENT PROPERTIES OF COGNITION

No study of composite figures is complete without some consideration of the influential essay published in 1942 by Rudolph Wittkower.[1] "Marvels of the East: A Study in the History of Monsters" documented the transmission of a particular style of ethnographic description (and depiction) from its earliest known sources in hand-copied manuscripts of the fourth century BC to the age of the printing press. The monsters in question fall mostly under my definition of "composites." They are thought to have entered Greek literature as borrowings from Sanskrit fables, carried by ambassadors to the courts of Persia and India.[2] In the bestiaries of medieval Europe, they came to define India, in particular, as a land of exotic marvels. Their compound bodies, comprising accurately depicted parts from diverse species, were copied there in conventional forms. The makers of these fantastic beasts acted more as reproducers than innovators, holding in check their imaginations and faithfully rendering the antique prototypes.[3] And after the sixteenth century AD, when travel to India became increasingly common, European visitors continued to "see" the same bizarre creatures, illustrating their experiences with resolute confidence.[4]

This apparent failure of perception or, as he termed it, the monster's remarkable "power of survival," was a central concern of

Wittkower's essay. To account for it, he invoked an acquired defect of the "occidental mentality," describing the latter as "fettered by classical accounts" and unable to represent the East as anything more than a static repository of imaginary otherness. Yet as he himself noted, the same composite creatures also migrated eastward, via Byzantium, appearing in al-Qazwini's thirteenth-century cosmography, which includes images of dog-headed humans (or "cynocephali") comparable to those on the Hereford *mappa mundi*. Others had their remote origins in the ancient Near East, where—as discussed in the preceding chapters—the deeper history of composites can be similarly associated with bureaucratic modes of thought, with the expanding frontiers of urban trading systems, and with the cosmopolitan face of elite culture.

At each twist and turn of the monster's tail, Wittkower confronted evidence for the confinement of these imaginary creatures to restricted and highly codified modes of image making and image circulation—first within the high-elite sphere of courtly interaction, and later through the more widely disseminated (but still tightly controlled) medium of reproductive prints. He nevertheless insisted on their cultural and cognitive universality. "Monsters," he confidently wrote, "composite beings, half-human, half-animal—play a part in the thought and imagery of all people at all times."[5] Claims of this sort have been rehearsed many times in the course of this book. As I hope to have shown, they are more often repeated than demonstrated. Nor can they be easily reconciled with the extensive apparatus, institutional and technological, that so often lies behind the making of composite figures, both modern and ancient, and on which they seem so often to depend for their circulation.

An archaeological perspective allows us to release the composite figure from the spell of the primordial, which surrounds the more vague concept of the "monstrous." Its origins *as a stable and widely transmitted type of image* belong to the first age of mechanical reproduction, beginning around six thousand years ago. And its underlying logic of figuration—based on the extraction of standard subunits from their given frames and their recombination into composite wholes—expresses modes of practical and abstract reasoning that underpinned the growth of large-scale social formations. Within such contexts, the counterfactual properties of composite figures were offset against two distinct forms of intuitive knowledge, one universal and the other historically contingent.

The first type of knowledge allows properties of vitality and movement to be attributed unreflectively to artificial composites, based on the mind's innate tendency to compensate for gaps and absences in the visible world, conjuring organic-seeming wholes out of ill-fitting parts. This capacity is presumably universal and can be considered a part of "intuitive biology," but it was little exploited in the pictorial arts of early hunter-gatherer and farming populations, which focused on the representation of living things that can be seen in the world. The second type of intuitive knowledge, within which the counterfactual properties of composites were grounded, is a historical product of technological and institutional environments that came into existence at a relatively recent point in evolutionary time, with the emergence of the first cities and state-like systems of organization. Such settings fostered the cultivation of an otherwise latent mode of perception that confronts the world, not as we usually encounter it—composed of unique and sentient totalities—but as a realm of divisible subjects, each comprising a multitude of fissionable and recombinable parts ("seeing like a state," as James C. Scott might have it).[6]

The embedding of composite figuration within this kind of "double-intuitive"—comprising both universal and historical aspects of cognition—laid foundations for the enhanced orders of cultural receptivity predicted by an "epidemiological" approach. The specific distribution of composite figures in the visual record must be further situated, however, within the institutional dynamics of elite culture, and within particular strategies of governance that first took root during the Bronze Age, including the dissemination of officially sanctioned images through mechanical reproduction. What then remains of the basic hypothesis with which I began: that as minimally counterintuitive images, depictions of fantastic, composite animals should exhibit special properties of cultural transmission?

I suggest we can still accept, with the evolutionary psychologists, that the transmission of cultural imaginaries within a given population is grounded in frameworks of inference that are intuitively shared by most of its members. But it is only in view of the unique plasticity of human cognition—its embedding within forms of practical reason; its ability to shape and be shaped by institutional environments constructed over historical rather than genetic timescales—that the value of this insight becomes clear. The basic point has been well made by Michael Tomasello:

> For human cognitive functions shared with other mammals and primates, there has been plenty of time for biological evolution to work its wonders. But for uniquely human cognitive functions, there has been insufficient time for a whole host of these—only 6 million years at most, but much more likely only one-quarter of a million years. A much more plausible view is thus one that focuses on processes that work much more quickly—in historical and ontogenetic time, for example—and searches for the ways in which these processes actually go about creating and maintaining uniquely human cognitive functions.

As he goes on to state:

> The basic problem with genetically based modularity approaches—especially when they address uniquely human and socially constituted artifacts and social practices—is that they attempt to skip from the first page of the story, genetics, to the last page of the story, current human cognition, without going through any of the intervening pages. These theorists are thus in many cases leaving out of account formative elements

in both historical and ontogenetic time that intervene between the human genotype and phenotype.[7]

The early history of composite figuration demonstrates how these "formative elements" of cognition may result from complex conjunctures of social, technological, and moral processes. Conjunctures of that sort cannot be replicated in a modern experimental setting. They belong to the irreversible flow of historical time. It is partly in reconstructing such emergent properties of cognition that an archaeological—rather than laboratory-based or ethnographic—approach remains fundamental to the understanding of cultural transmission and cultural change.

NOTES

INTRODUCTION

1. Benjamin 1999 [1936].

2. Frankfort 1939.

3. Monsters, variously defined, have long been a favorite topic in cultural and literary studies, where they have been considered as symbolic expressions of social difference or moral corruption (Lenfant 1999; Strickland 2003), as metaphors of geographical and cultural remoteness (Wittkower 1942; Mitter 1992; Romm 1992), or as public responses to the disturbing effects of new technologies, especially those that challenge established classifications of the empirical world (Graf 1999; Smits 2006; and for more wide-ranging studies, see Cohen 1996; Bildhauer and Mills 2003; Asma 2009). By contrast, the focus here will be on the transmission of images, confined to a study of composite animals, which I will go on to define in terms that are visual and technical, rather than moral or psychological.

4. For example, Sperber 1985, 1996; Boyer 1994, 2001.

5. Stafford 2007: 2.

6. Mesoudi et al. 2006.

7. For a sample of current applications of cognitive psychology in archaeology, see the collected papers in Renfrew and Scarre 1998; Renfrew, Frith, and Malfouris 2009.

8. Scott and Baron-Cohen 1996.

9. Mithen 1998a, especially pp. 172–173; and cf. Mithen 1998b; Boyer 2001: 323–324.

10. Hallowell 1955.

11. Leevers and Harris 1998; and see also Low et al. 2009.

12. Take Baxandall, for example, on Renaissance art: "To sum up: some of the mental equipment a man orders his visual experience with is variable, and much of this variable equipment is culturally relative, in the sense of being determined by the society which has influenced his experience. Among

these variables are categories with which he classifies his visual stimuli, the knowledge he will use to supplement what his immediate vision gives him, and the attitude he will adopt to the kind of artificial object seen. . . . Whatever his own specialized professional skills, he is himself a member of the society he works for and shares its visual experience and habit" (1988: 40).

13. Quack 2009.

14. See Atran 1990; Atran and Medin 2008.

15. Küchler 2005.

16. Küchler 2005: 207.

17. Küchler 2002; Stafford 2007; see also Melion and Küchler 1991; Belting 2005.

18. Sperber 1996b.

19. Rostovtzeff 1922: 192.

CHAPTER 1

1. Rostovtzeff 1926b, 1941.

2. Bowersock 1974: 19.

3. The terms of that debate are usefully outlined in Sherratt and Sherratt 1998.

4. For intellectual assessments, see Reinhold 1946; Momigliano 1994 [1952]. For biographical insights, see Wes 1990.

5. A recent revival of public interest in the ancient art of the Eurasian steppe can be attributed in part to remarkable discoveries in the Filippovka kurgans of the southern Urals, reviewed in Yablonsky 2010. Major exhibitions have been mounted (see Aruz 2000; Parzinger 2007); and for related discussions of "animal style" art and its interregional connections, see Aruz et al. 2006.

6. In addition to Rostovtzeff 1922 and 1929, see his (1926a) *A History of the Ancient World, Volume 1: The Orient and Greece*.

7. See especially the concluding chapter (9) of *Iranians and Greeks*, which considers the origins of the Russian state on the Dnieper; Rostovtzeff 1922: 210–222.

8. Rostovtzeff 1920.

9. Rostovtzeff 1932: 6–7.

10. For example, Childe 1936; Frankfort 1932.

11. See Riegl 1893 (English translation, 1992); and for further discussion, Gombrich 1984; Iversen 1993.

12. Elsner 2006.

13. Riegl 2000 [1900]: 124.

14. Poulsen 1912. For recent perspectives on the concept of "orientaliza-tion" in the Iron Age Mediterranean, see Riva and Vella 2006; and for a focused treatment of "oriental" monsters in Corinthian vase-painting, and their role in the definition of Greek cultural identity during the seventh and sixth centuries BC, see Winkler-Horaček 2011.

15. Meyer Schapiro (2000 [1936]) took Riegl's intellectual disciples to task for treating visual styles as cultural proxies for "racial-psychological" constants.

16. For the *Kulturkreislehre*, see Andriolo (1979), and for "hyper-diffusionism" see Trigger 1989: 150–155.

17. Momigliano (1994: 43) suggests that "Rostovtzeff, although he stud-ied ancient religion, can hardly be said to have been aware of the profound impact that the religious needs of man have had upon his development."

18. Rostovtzeff 1922: 192.

19. Ibid.

20. See, more recently, Gunter 2009.

21. Rostovtzeff 1922: 192–193.

22. Ibid., 193–209.

CHAPTER 2

1. Davidoff and Roberson 2002; and for evidence that animal behavior in general holds a special command over human visual attention, see also New et al. 2007.

2. Stafford 2007: 43–73; and see also Clark 1997: 167–169.

3. Sperber 1985, 1996a, with further references.

4. Further discussion of neo-Darwinian approaches to cultural transmis-sion, and their applications in archaeology and anthropology, can be found in Shennan 2002; Richerson and Boyd 2005. G.E.R. Lloyd (2007) considers the findings of evolutionary psychology—which represents just one strand of neo-Darwinian theory—in relation to case studies from ancient Greece and China, comparing their respective classifications of natural kinds, emo-tions, and modes of causality. Brian Boyd (2009) explores the implication of similar theories for the development of art and fictional narrative, from prehistory to the present.

5. Sperber 1996a: 2, 25, 58; cf. Boyer 2000: 196.

6. Ibid., pp. 2, 64–65, 82.

7. See Hirschfeld and Gelman, eds., 1994, and further references following.

8. For example, Pinker 1994; Dehaene 1997; Kanwisher et al. 1997.

9. For example, Scholl and Leslie 1999.

10. For a review of current issues, see Barrett and Kurzban 2006; also Boyer, ed., 1992. For a critical perspective on modularity and its implications for the relationship between cognition and culture, see Tomasello 1999, especially pp. 201–217.

11. Sperber and Hirschfeld 2004: 41–42.

12. Berlin 1992.

13. Atran 1990; Atran and Medin 2008; but for other possibilities, see Carey 1985; Carey and Spelke 1994.

14. Sperber and Hirschfeld 2004: 43.

15. For example, Boyer 1994, 2000, and 2001, with explicit discussion of "counterintuitive biology" and its role in the transmission of supernatural concepts (pp. 75–79).

16. Boyer 1994: 122. Pyysiäinen (2001), Atran (2002), and Barrett (2004) develop partially comparable approaches to the analysis of religion, and offer useful commentaries on Boyer, but a full review of this literature is beyond the scope of the present study.

17. Sperber and Hirschfeld 2004: 44.

18. See Boyer 1994: 118–119; 2000; Sperber and Hirschfeld 2004: 45.

19. Stafford 2007: 71.

20. Sperber 1996b.

21. Arnheim 1966: 256–257.

22. Lenfant (1999: 198) notes that the corresponding Greek term is "*teras*, which originally had, just like *monstrum*, the special meaning of a divine sign, a 'portent,' with different sorts of referents"; and also "specifically designated mythological monsters (like Cerberus or the Sphinx) and actual monstrous births."

23. Sonik (2010) provides detailed consideration of this point in relation to (mainly literary) sources from ancient Mesopotamia.

24. Descola 2010; Karadimas 2010.

25. Descola would see the regular depiction of composites as reflecting a more general set of ontological principles, for which he coins the term "analogistic" (see also Descola 2005). Intriguingly, his examples of analogism derive almost exclusively from large-scale, hierarchical societies including Han China, medieval Europe, and the recent historical kingdoms of West Africa. Neither Descola nor Karadimas, however, propose any causal

or historical relationship between analogistic ontologies and processes of state formation.

26. See Descola 2010: 168.

27. Richter 2008 [1952]: 160.

28. Arnheim 1966: 256.

29. Rudenko 1970.

30. Napier 1986: 52.

31. See Ingold 2000; Descola 2010.

32. Invoking a *tupilak* was, for Inuit, an act of sorcery carried out in private, and most effectively by shamans. It allowed the harmful spirit not only to pursue a named individual but also to take on the forms and capacities of various animals in doing so. It is important to emphasize that the *tupilak* effigy was not, in origin, a permanent image, but an ephemeral assemblage of bones, to which a piece of clothing from the intended victim might be added. The open and public carving of durable *tupilak* sculptures is, by contrast, a modern practice, responding to the influence of missionization (which assimilated the *tupilak* to devil-worship) and also to the commercial demands of tourism and the European art market; see Rasmussen 1921; Petersen 1964; Auger 2005.

33. Guenther 1999; and for the story of "The Mantis Assumes the Form of a Hartebeest," see Bleek and Lloyd 1911: 2–17.

34. For example, Descola 2010: 12, fig. 1; 26–32, figs. 10–11.

35. See Canetti 2000 [1960]: 337–384. Relevant here is Victor Turner's (1969: 107) analysis of ritual temporalities, and how a phase within a rite of passage can be transformed—within large-scale social formations—into the durable instantiation of "liminal beings." The fixing of ritual values within stable media of transmission is also considered—albeit from very different perspectives—in the work of Ruth Benedict (1935), Fredrik Barth (1990), and Harvey Whitehouse (2004); and see also the following, chapter 5.

CHAPTER 3

1. Mithen 1998a: 173; and see, similarly, Borić 2007: 97.

2. Accessible overviews are provided by Bahn and Vertut 1988; White 2003; and for more detailed consideration of methodological issues in the interpretation of Paleolithic art, see Conkey et al. 1997.

3. The occurrence of "therianthropes"—or part human, part animal figures—in Paleolithic rock art has been widely linked to debates concerning the origins of shamanism (for example, Makkay 1953; Lommel 1967; and

for an early critique, see Leroi-Gourhan 1977). The development of these debates, and their recent revitalization through the work of David Lewis-Williams and others, is usefully reviewed in Ronald Hutton's (2001) *Shamans: Siberian Spirituality and the Western Imagination* (see especially pp. 130–133; and also de Beaune 1998).

4. Schmid 1989.

5. See Hahn 1986.

6. Conard 2003.

7. For instance, R. Dale Guthrie's (2005: 446) reading of the Hohlenstein Stadel "lion-man" as a standing bear.

8. Taborin et al. 2001.

9. See Breuil 1952.

10. Breuil's approach is placed in its intellectual and historical context by Ucko and Rosenfeld 1967.

11. Bahn and Vertut 1988: 42.

12. Ucko and Rosenfeld 1967: 204–206.

13. See, for instance, Guthrie 2005: 100–101.

14. Lewis-Williams 2002; and see also Clottes and Lewis-Williams 1998. In making their case, these authors also draw attention to a range of other factors, including the special sensory environment of caves and its conduciveness to altered states of consciousness; the rendering of animal forms from natural features in cave walls (perhaps implying an artificially heightened state of visual awareness); and the presence in Upper Paleolithic rock art of "entoptic" images: geometric patterns produced by the nervous system under circumstances of sensory deprivation and/or altered consciousness. For critical commentaries on their interpretation of these features, see Bahn 1997; Layton 2000.

15. Attributing the "explosion" of representational art in the Upper Paleolithic period to a shift in human cognitive capacities may be unnecessary in view of other, more parsimonious explanations. Powell et al. (2009) argue, for instance, that the first widespread attestation of modern symbolic behavior in the archaeological record is best explained by demographic factors (that is, changing densities of human populations and related transmission rates for culturally inherited skills); cf. White 1992. Mithen's interpretation also rests on the problematic assumption that neurological disorders in autistic children can be used to develop inferences about premodern modes of cognition (see the introduction to this volume for further references).

16. For example, Clottes and Lewis-Williams 1998: 17–19, figs. 10–12.

17. Jolly (2002) estimates that figures composed of mixed human and animal attributes constitute no more than 3 to 4 percent of painted subjects in the known corpus of southern African rock art. Anne Solomon (1997) notes that the date at which figures with composite anatomy began to be depicted in San rock art is itself unknown, and that indigenous accounts link such figures more closely to the ancestral dead than to shamanic trance-states.

18. For example, those of the Natufian or Epipaleolithic period (ca. 11,000–9000 BC) in the southern Levant (see Perrot and Ladiray 1988: 58–59, fig. 32, pl. xxv; and Grosman et al. 2008), and their European counterparts such as the Mesolithic burial of a woman adorned with deer antlers and other animal ornamentation, discovered in Bad Dürrenberg in 1934 and dating to between ca. 7000 and 6200 BC, now displayed at the Landesmuseum für Vorgeschichte in Halle (Saale; see Geupel 1977).

19. McCown 1937; Vandermeersch 1970. Direct evidence for the use of wings from predatory birds as ritual costume derives from Zawi Chemi Shanidar in northern Iraq (ca. 11,000–10,000 BC; Solecki 1977; and for recent discussion, see Mithen 2003: 420–422).

20. Composite burials, using the horns of cattle rather than gazelle to adorn human corpses, became a common feature of Neolithic funerary rituals in the Nile Valley from around 6000 to 4000 BC (Wengrow 2006: 56–59). Of the many Neolithic examples that might be cited from Southwest Asia, the inclusion of a plastered human skull alongside the headless body of a gazelle is particularly striking (Goring-Morris and Kolska Horwitz 2007). The assemblage was sealed beneath a floor around 10,000 years ago at the site of Kfar Ha-Horesh, in the Jezreel Valley of northern Israel. For the famous "Puyang shaman" burial of Neolithic China (Yangshao culture, Henan Province), see Kesner 1991: 36, 45, with further references.

21. Wengrow (2006) provides a synthetic treatment of the later prehistory of Egypt; for Southwest Asia, see Charvát 2002.

22. For a global survey of the origins and spread of farming, see Bellwood 2005.

23. Cauvin 1994 (English translation, 2000).

24. Hodder 2006: 142; Borić 2007; Meskell 2008.

25. See Meskell and Nakamura 2009; Hodder and Meskell 2010: 61.

26. Schmidt 2006: 210–218.

27. Wengrow 2001a, 2003; Helmer et al. 2004.

28. Gifford Gonzalez 2007.

29. Russell and McGowan 2003.

30. For discussion of an isolated and ambiguous exception, see Borić 2007: 96–97. Ian Hodder and Lynn Meskell suggest that schematic clay figurines with pinched-out faces might have been intended to encapsulate both avian and human qualities, and propose tentative analogies at the much earlier site of Göbekli Tepe. But they also note that "hybrid human forms are not common overall at Çatalhöyük or elsewhere in the Neolithic of the Middle East" (Hodder and Meskell 2010: 61; cf. Meskell and Nakamura 2009). Carolyn Nakamura, working on the same corpus of imagery, is more categorical, stating that "there are no clear examples of human-animal hybrids," and drawing a suggestive contrast with the interplay of human and animal body parts in domestic rituals and burials (Nakamura 2010: 309).

31. Mallowan and Rose 1935; Goff 1963; Wengrow 2001b. For a remarkable, but also strikingly isolated, exception to this pattern, see the richly decorated Halaf-period vessel discussed in detail by Breniquet 1992.

32. Madjidzadeh 2008.

33. Oates 1966, 1978; Yoffee and Clark, eds., 1993; Wengrow 1998.

34. Wengrow 2006: 41–62.

35. Hendrickx and Vermeersch 2000.

36. Wengrow 2006: 41–62.

37. Flores 2003; Hoffman et al. 1982: 55–59.

38. R. F. Friedman 2008.

39. Van Neer et al. 2004. The cemetery, known as HK6, remained in use for human burials throughout the fourth millennium, but those of wild animals belong only to the Naqada I–II periods (ca. 4000–3300 BC).

40. R. F. Friedman 1996; Linseele and van Neer 2003.

41. Wengrow 2006: 99–123.

42. Dreyer et al. 2003: 72–75, 80–84, pl. 15: a–b.

43. Flinders Petrie's (1921) White Cross-Lined or C-Ware.

44. See Wengrow 2006: 102–108; and for an alternative view, see Hendrickx 1998.

45. Only a slim portion of the designs on the Abydos vases would have been visible at any one time, and turning the vessel was therefore necessary to gain a full prospectus of any single animal. The general orientation of the figures, and the lines linking them, further encourage the viewer to follow a horizontal axis around the vessel surface, maintaining an interplay between images recalled (as they disappear from sight) and images brought to mind (as they enter the field of vision).

46. Petrie's (1921) Decorated or D-Ware; see also Wengrow and Baines 2004.

47. A contrast can be drawn here with the more complex subdivision of bodies, and more detailed rendering of technological details, on an extensive painting (ca. 3500 BC) that covered the plastered walls of a large mud-brick tomb at Hierakonpolis (Case and Payne 1962). Modes of depiction thus varied between contexts and media. Carvings and pecked images on rock surfaces of the Eastern and Western Deserts may present another perspective on predynastic depiction, but ongoing difficulties with their dating preclude any definitive statement on the matter (Wengrow 2006: 111–114).

48. Ciałowicz 1991.

49. Van Lepp 1999.

50. Baumgartel 1960: 85–86.

51. Needler 1984: 336–343, cat. 267–273.

CHAPTER 4

1. Boyer 2000: 196.

2. For the concept of cultural ecology, see Bateson 1972; and for its application to images, see Gombrich 1998.

3. For a detailed account, see Wengrow 2006: 127–217.

4. Asselberghs 1961.

5. Boehmer 1974a, 1974b.

6. Moorey 1987; Philip 2002.

7. See also Baines 1995.

8. Weeks 1971: 80, and see also pp. 76–88.

9. For example, Fischer 1958; Churcher 1984.

10. For the adaptation of Mesopotamian composites in Egyptian art of the protodynastic periods, see the following, notes 36–38. For examples and discussion of locally invented composites, see McDonald 2000; Huyge 2004.

11. Robins 1994: 13.

12. Ibid.; and see also Baines 2007: 218–219.

13. Schäfer [1919] 1986.

14. Fischer 1978.

15. Eckmann and Shafik 2005; Hill 2007.

16. Frankfort 1948: 12; Hornung 1982: 109–125; 2000. Anatomical specificities, beyond what was needed to convey the essential components of an image, seem to have been consciously avoided for figures associated with the gods (whether human, animal, or mixed), perhaps because they implied a proximity to the visible world that was considered inappropriate in such

contexts. For depictions of bodies that approached or contained divine agency, including those of royalty in certain contexts, many details of musculature may be either deliberately lacking or hidden by uniform clothing; cf. Hornung 1982: 107–109; Baines 2007: 219, n.13.

17. Szpakowska 2009; Lucarelli 2010. For reasons unclear, the protective images of *Bes* and *Taweret*—beings part-divine, part-demonic, and both associated with the domestic sphere—were regularly depicted with heightened anatomical definition, lending a distinct veracity to their fantastic, composite forms.

18. Kroeper and Krzyżaniak 1992.

19. C. A. Ward 2003.

20. Frankfort 1941.

21. Emery 1961: 216–222; Gale et al. 2000: 358–365.

22. Emery 1961: 241–242; Killen 1980.

23. Whitehouse 2002: 427, 432–434; see also Bussmann 2010.

24. Petrie et al. 1913: 23–24, pls. 8–9; cf. Wengrow 2006: 169.

25. Hodder 2011.

26. Comparative discussion of the origins and early development of Egyptian, Mesopotamian, and Iranian scripts can be found in Houston, ed., 2004; for the Indus script, see also Parpola 1994.

27. For more extended surveys, see Aruz, ed., 2003; Wengrow 2010b. For discussion of particular Bronze Age societies in the Near East, see Akkermans and Schwartz 2003 (Syria); Kohl 2007 (Central Asia); Pollock 1999 (Mesopotamia); Possehl 2002 (Indus Valley); D. T. Potts 1990 (Arabian Peninsula), 1999 (western Iran).

28. The geographical distribution of metals and other raw materials, and its relationship to the early growth of urban life and long-distance trade in the western Old World, is discussed at greater length by Moorey 1994 and D. T. Potts 1997; see also Sherratt and Sherratt 1991.

29. Algaze 1993; Wengrow 2006: 13–40.

30. T. F. Potts 1994.

31. Crawford 1998.

32. Pettinato 1991.

33. Possehl 2002.

34. Kohl 2007.

35. Dickinson 1994; Parkinson and Galaty, eds., 2010.

36. For the initial appearance of both composite types on cylinder seals in Mesopotamia and western Iran, see Frankfort 1939: 25–27; Brandes 1979; Amiet 1972, 1980: 75; Dittmann 1986; Moorey 1987.

37. According to Fischer (1987: 15), the Mesopotamian origin of the serpent-necked felines on the Narmer Palette was first, and independently, noted by L. Heuzey and A. Weigall in the late nineteenth and early twentieth centuries. Frankfort (1951: 109) listed "composite animals, especially winged griffins and serpent-necked felines, on palettes and knife-handles" among those cultural elements imported to Egypt from Mesopotamia in the late fourth millennium BC (see further, Boehmer 1974b; Kantor 1992; Pittman 1994; and for the broadly contemporaneous execution of composite figures, including a seated griffin, in miniature three-dimensional sculpture, see Ciałowicz 2007).

38. Quibell 1898; Kaiser 1990; Wengrow 2006: 41. A similar arrangement of serpent-necked felines, carved in relief, is found on a palette from Minshat Ezzat in the Nile delta (el-Baghdadi 1999). The origin of these composite animal designs in seal carving can be indirectly demonstrated only through comparison with cylinder seals found outside Egypt, notably on the lower and middle reaches of the Euphrates, and at Susa in southwest Iran (Boehmer 1974b; Teissier 1987; Pittman 1996).

39. The protective goddess *Taweret* was visualized in Egypt as a complex animal composite, comprising a standing figure with hippopotamus head, leonine claws and feet, and a crocodile's back and tail (Gundlach 1986). On apotropaic ivory wands of the Middle Kingdom (ca. 2000–1650 BC), she is depicted with knife in hand or claws extended, marching alongside other protective figures (Altenmüller 1983, 1986). The latter include the serpent-necked felines of the much earlier Narmer Palette (notes 37 and 38, earlier), which are otherwise undocumented between the protodynastic period and the Middle Kingdom. This would suggest a lost medium (or media) of transmission for such images, probably including woven textiles, the appearance of which may be echoed in tomb paintings at Beni Hassan and el-Bersha (ca. 1900 BC), where fantastic creatures appear alongside ordinary desert animals (Newberry 1893, 1895; cf. Fischer 1987: 16). The core elements of *Taweret*'s image are attested in amulet form by the late Old Kingdom (Petrie 1914: 47, pl. xl; Dubiel 2008) and are depicted on scarab seals by the First Intermediate Period (W. A. Ward 1978: 53, pl. 6: 180). The apotropaic function of this composite figure and its association with women and childbirth in Egypt are discussed by Altenmüller (1965) and, in the context of domestic religion, by Sadek (1987: 125–127) and Stevens (2009).

40. The transmission of *Taweret*'s figure to the Aegean, and its transformation there into the Middle Minoan "genius," is the subject of a monograph by J. Weingarten (1991; see also Hallager and Weingarten 1993; Phillips

2008: 156–167; Weingarten 2010). For the likelihood of a Levantine route of transmission, see Kemp and Merrillees 1980: 268–286; Lambrou-Phillipson 1991; Wengrow 2010a); for evidence of *Taweret* imagery at Byblos (Lebanon) in the Middle Bronze Age, see Aruz 2008b: 136–137; and for fuller discussion of evidence from Aegean seals, see Krzyszkowska 2005. Broader, and highly divergent, assessments of the scope and impact of Egyptian/Levantine introductions to Early and Middle Minoan Crete are provided by Warren 1995; Watrous 2004; Schoep 2006; and Cherry 2010.

41. Mellink (1987) makes a case for Anatolian influences on the development of the Minoan genius, based on comparisons with *karum*-period and Old Hittite seal carving.

42. No statement on the chronological priority of one imported motif over another should be taken as categorical, since many media of transmission are undoubtedly missing from the surviving body of evidence. In his "Notes on the Cretan Griffin," Frankfort (1936: 216–217) stressed the likely importance of ornamented textiles—echoes of which are found in the decoration of Minoan miniature frescoes—in the transfer of fantastic animal images, notably the winged griffin and sphinx (see also Morgan 1988: 49–51; Crowley 1989: 40–53; Frankfort 1996: 263–264; Aruz 2008a: 106–108). Recent studies emphasize Egypt as a source of imagery on palatial Crete (Karetsou et al., eds., 2001), but like the technique of fresco painting itself, imaginary creatures may be better considered part of what Susan Sherratt (1994: 237) terms an "elite *koiné*—artistic, iconographical, ideological, technological," widely shared among the palatial centres of the Eastern Mediterranean seaboard in the mid- to late second millennium BC (cf. Feldman 2006: 67–68, 2007); and see the following, chapter 6, on "integrative modes."

43. Early attestations of the griffin on the Greek mainland derive from gold inlays and ornamented weaponry in the Mycenaean Shaft Graves (ca. 1600–1500 BC), where it appears on sword- and dagger-blades in the "flying gallop" pose (Karo 1930; Morgan 1988: 51–52). Morgan (1988: 53) notes a recurrent nexus of visual associations between griffins, lions, and the prowess of male warriors in the elite imagery of Late Bronze Age Greece, with parallels to the east in objects such as a decorated axe-blade of Ahmose I from Thebes (ca. 1570–1545 BC), and later on ivories found at sites along the Cypriot and Levantine coasts (ca. 1300–1100 BC; cf. Kantor 1956). In the Late Bronze Age Aegean, leashed griffins are depicted on seals in the service of anthropomorphic figures. A protective function is further implied by their location around the carved throne at Knossos, as reconstructed by

Arthur Evans (cf. Feldman 2006: 80–81). Griffins also appear, alongside lions, around the throne in wall paintings at Mycenaean Pylos (Immerwahr 1990: 136, pl. 79, and see p. 137 [and also Crowley 2008: 270, 279] for possible sphinxes in the decorative programme at Tiryns; and figure 6.1, later).

44. Parpola 1994; Possehl 2002. Among the most common motifs on Indus seals is the unicorn, also a subject of depiction in terracotta figurines (Kenoyer 1998: 87–88). For its status as a "fabulous animal" and possible derivation from West Asian prototypes, see Parpola 2011.

45. Al-Sindī 1999.

46. Sarianidi 1981; Francfort 1994; Aruz 1999.

47. See Frankfort 1939; Pittman 1995.

48. Amiet 1966, 1972; Roach 2009.

49. Pittman 1994.

50. Pittman 1997.

51. Serpent-necked felines are documented on seal impressions from the site of Habuba Kabira, on the Middle Euphrates, with close connections to the much larger urban centers of the southern Mesopotamian alluvium (Amiet 1980: 505, pl. 123: 1631). The seal repertory from Tel Brak, an early urban center on the Syrian steppe, includes the image of a standing figure with feline head and tail, as yet without parallel (Oates and Oates 1997: 294, fig. 14).

52. Akkermans and Schwartz 2003: 210–224 (Ninevite 5 culture); Rova and Weiss, eds., 2003.

53. Matthiae et al., eds., 1995; Akkermans and Schwartz 2003: 232–287; Margueron 2004.

54. Porada 1985; Matthiae 2003.

55. See Frankfort 1939: 308; Barber 1991; Sherratt and Sherratt 1991; and notes 39 and 42, earlier.

56. Jasim and Oates 1986; Nissen 2001; Oates 1993; Wengrow 1998: 790–792.

57. Wengrow 2001b.

58. McAdam 2003: 183; cf. Moorey 2003: 19–20.

59. Wickede 1990; Pittman 2001.

60. Wickede 1990; Pittman 2001; and see also Caldwell 1976.

61. Amiet 1980; Pittman 2001: 412–415; Cool Root 2005: cat. 114, 115.

62. Potts 1997: 138–163; Rova 2008: 24.

63. Nissen et al. 1993.

64. Nissen et al. 1993: 14, 30.

65. Englund 1998: 171–172.

66. Brandes 1986; Frankfort 1996. Schematic modes of representation remained in use for certain purposes, but are now instantly distinguishable from the detailed renderings of animal and human figures, which often appear in complex poses and extended narrative scenes; see Amiet 1980; Brandes 1979; Schmandt-Besserat 1993.

67. Dittmann 1986; Nissen 1977; Nissen et al. 1993: 15–18.

68. Stafford 2007: 45.

CHAPTER 5

1. First millennium BC versions of the text have been found at Nineveh, Assur, and Uruk; Köcher 1953; Wiggermann 1992; Herles 2006: 185–186.

2. Wiggermann 1996: 219; see also Radner 2005: 548–549.

3. Wiggermann, in Porada 1995: 84.

4. Weingarten 1983; Müller and Pini, eds., 1998; Krzyszkowska 2005: 150–153, 178–185, with divergent views from Weingarten on the replication of seal designs; and for the latter, see also Weingarten 1986. Schlager (1996) proposes a paleontological inspiration for at least some the fantastic composites among the Zakros sealings.

5. Hopkins 1934, 1961; Kantor 1962; Napier 1986: 91–124.

6. Vernant 1991: 137.

7. Napier 1990: 77–111.

8. Boardman 2002: 51–52; cf. Graf 1999.

9. Kostoula and Maran 2012.

10. Zuckerman 2008, with further references.

11. Kostoula and Maran 2012; cf. Karageorghis 1993: 33–35; pl. 20: 4–5, 7; Webb 1999: 219–222; and for Near Eastern parallels, Wilcke 1972–1975: 530–535.

12. Karageorghis (1993: 35) notes that Late Cypriote III terracotta masks found at Enkomi and Kition are too small and impractical for wearing, and most likely replicate the appearance of functional masks in perishable materials such as leather or wood.

13. Carter 1987; for a comparison with gorgon-like helmets from late eighth or seventh century BC Tiryns, see Napier 1986: 86, pl. 34.

14. Moorey 1975; Auerbach 1994.

15. For general surveys, see Frankfort 1939 (cylinder seals); Moorey 2003: 22–46 (terracotta molds).

16. See Moorey 2003: 28.

17. Sax and Meeks 1994.

18. See Eisenstein 1983.

19. See Yoffee 2005.

20. Gombrich 1984: 256.

21. In Mesopotamia, stamp seals were widely used in late Neolithic villages long prior to the beginning of urban life. Until the fifth millennium BC, however, they carried mainly nonfigurative designs; Wickede 1990.

22. A similar hypothesis has been advanced more recently by Steven Mithen (2001: 49): "We can all sit and day-dream and think of fantastical monsters; but to describe that monster to someone else, or recall it yourself the following day is not so easy—unless the basic idea is offloaded from the mind into the physical world, as by drawing a picture or making some notes. Such ideas are difficult for minds to remember, to manipulate, and to communicate, because they do not correspond to a part of our evolved psychology. Contrast this with thinking about, say, some gossip concerning an acquaintance. That is always easy to remember and to pass on. This is because it engages with a part of our evolved psychology—the ideas in gossip are exactly the types of ideas our minds have evolved to deal with. In contrast, ideas about monsters and supernatural beings have no natural home within the mind." Like the earlier views of Gombrich, these assertions have no apparent basis in cognitive-experimental data. Such data as exists in fact tends to support the opposite view, that representations that explicitly violate some limited aspect of domain-specific knowledge are inherently more memorable and "catchy" than ordinary, intuitive ones (Boyer and Ramble 2001).

23. The point could be equally well made in relation to ethnographically documented counterexamples, such as the monster masks of the Pacific Northwest, famously analyzed by Claude Lévi-Strauss (1982).

24. Chang 1963, 1983: 56–80; Falkenhausen 2006.

25. Chang 1999: 49–52; Zhongpei 2005.

26. Among the latter, found at Banpo in Shaanxi Province, is a recurrent image interpreted as "a human face with a fish design at each ear" (Chang 1983: 114; Zhongpei 2005: 62, fig. 3.33); attempts have been made to link this design to the practice of shamanism (Marilyn Fu, cited by Chang 1983: 114).

27. Bagley 2008: 85–92.

28. Keightley 1998.

29. Falkenhausen 2006.

30. For which, see Bagley 2008.

31. Rostovtzeff 1929: 70–73.

32. Bagley 2006.

33. For example, Kesner 1991: 36, 45, with further references.

34. Bagley 2006: 17.

35. Bagley 1990.

36. And compare Gell 1998: 73–90.

37. Ledderose 2000: 34. Rawson (1987: 28) suggests that the elements of the *taotie* and also of the *long* dragon may have been specifically devised "to fill compartments of different shapes and proportions on angular and highly articulated vessels." "Imaginary beasts," she notes, "were much easier to use in this way than real creatures, as they could be extended or compressed, and could be given new heads or different bodies as the shapes of the vessels demanded."

38. For example, in the decoration of Erligang ceramic vessels (ca. 1500–1300 BC) with carved clay stamps; Wang Haicheng (forthcoming) notes that these decorated pots "imitated both the shape and the decoration of bronzes . . . [by means of] a technique never used in the bronze foundries. Erligang bronze casters never used stamps or pattern blocks. Each piece of a mould or model was individually carved by expert designers." And for general observations on the avoidance of mechanical replication in the decoration of Shang and Zhou bronzes, see Ledderose 2000: 25–41.

39. Bagley 1987: 37–45.

40. Experts disagree categorically on the manual procedures followed (compare Bagley 1987: 37–45, 2008: 113–120, to Ledderose 2000: 39–40; Nickel 2006; and see also Bagley 2009). All concur, however, that no mechanical technique was regularly used to replicate surface ornament on cast bronzes until the fifth century BC, or perhaps some few centuries earlier.

41. Ledderose 2000: 25.

42. Bagley 1993, 1996; Li Xiating and Liang Zhiming 1996.

43. Sher 1988; see also Di Cosmo 1999: 924–945; and earlier, chapter 1, on Rostovtzeff's views concerning the transmission of "animal style" ornament in Eurasia.

44. Bagley 2006: 24–26.

CHAPTER 6

1. For a discussion of "cycles of contingency" in developmental systems theory, see Oyama et al., eds., 2003.

2. Bevan 2007: 171.

3. For an overview of state formation in Archaic Greece, see Runciman 1982.

4. Osborne 1998: 43.

5. See also Napier 1986; Winkler-Horaček 2008, 2011. Adrienne Mayor (2000) makes the intriguing case that depictions of certain fantastic beasts (for example, the griffin) in Iron Age Greece were informed by encounters with fossil remains of long-extinct species, eroding from the surface of the landscape (and see also Schlager 1996). By her own admission, however, the argument has little to say about why imaginary creatures should have become popular subjects of depiction at particular times, or about what she herself describes as: "the obviously imaginary hybrids of Greek tradition like Pegasus (a horse with wings), the Sphinx (a winged lion with a woman's head), the Minotaur (a man with a bull's head), and the half-man, half-horse Centaurs" (Mayor 2000: 16; cf. Boardman 2002).

6. Johnston 1993: 11.

7. Whitley 1994.

8. Whitley 1988.

9. Irene Winter (1995) explores similar tensions in relation to the composition of Greek epic, and in particular the Homeric portrayal of Phoenician traders: "makers and merchants as opposed to warriors, associated with no gods or family ties, deceitful, disrespectful of accepted codes of hospitality and friendship, unbound by social constraints." This she reads as a literary projection "of the social and economic present, the becoming [Greek] 'self' . . . [imbued] with all of the ambivalence and discomfort, denial even, that contemporary Greeks must have felt about the changes that their society was presently undergoing" (1995: 261).

10. For protopalatial Crete, see Krzyszkowska 2005: 32, 90, 147–150; for Late Helladic Greece, see Lambrou-Phillipson 1990: 74; and also Salje (1990) for the Common Mitanni Style.

11. Hallager and Weingarten (1993: 12, n. 23) note that "*Taweret*'s entry into Crete may have been facilitated by an older Minoan set of ideas connected with the ritual handling of liquids," and that her introduction coincides, broadly, with that of the rhyton as a specialized pouring vessel for ritual libations; hence: "It seems that the importation of *Taweret*, with her interest in rites of purification, was a significant part of the conceptual expansion of liquid-pouring rites as represented by new cult assemblages as, for example, at MMIIB Malia and Phaistos" (ibid.).

12. Crowley (2008: 279) observes that griffins "are everywhere in Mycenaean art, shown in flying gallop pose on blades from the Mycenae Shaft Graves, attacking deer on the Athens pyxis, and doing guard duty with lions on frescoes by the Pylos throne"; see also Morgan 1988: 49–51.

13. Reisner, 1923, pl. 55; see also Bonnet, 2000.

14. Kendall 1997: 53–73; Török 2009: 152–153.

15. Wengrow 2006: 170–195, with further references.

16. Kantor 1997 [1947]; Smith 1965.

17. See Cohen and Westbrook 2000.

18. Feldman 2006: 67–68, 74, 78–81.

19. Feldman 2006: 78.

20. De Miroschedji 1973; Lamberg-Karlovsky 1988; and for the wider visual milieu of "intercultural style" chlorite vessels, see Amiet 1986.

21. Kohl 2001.

22. For a representative range of images, see Aruz 2003b. Bull-men composites are atypical; an example is found on an unprovenanced vessel fragment that was subsequently matched to an excavated fragment from Sin Temple at Khafaje, in eastern Iraq (Frankfort 1935: 48, figs. 54, 55; Pittman 2002).

23. Madjidzadeh 2003.

24. Kohl et al. 1979; Madjidzadeh and Pittman 2008.

25. Kohl 1978.

26. Bevan 2007: 175.

27. Zarins 1978; Potts 1990: 66–67, with further references.

28. Hansen and Dales 1962: 79 (with mistranslation of the inscription as "Inanna and the Serpent"; the correct reading is "[To] Inanna: Panun," the latter being the name of the individual making an offering; Goetze 1970: 42 [Inscription: 7N-120]; my thanks to Gianni Marchesi and Piotr Steinkeller for these references, and to Andrew George for assistance).

29. Wiggermann 1992.

30. Wiggermann 1992: xii.

31. Porada 1995: 64.

32. See also Gurney 1935; Scurlock 2006.

33. See Gunter 2009; and for the influence of Neo-Assyrian composites on the elite art of Urartu (eastern Anatolia/southern Caucasus) in the early first millennium BC, see also Green 1994: 262–264.

34. Van Buren 1931; Klengel-Brandt 1968; Rittig 1977; Nakamura 2004.

35. Green 1983; Ornan 2004.

36. Wiggermann 1994: 225–226; Green 1994: 248–262; and also Black and Green 1992.

37. Wiggermann 1992: 56–66.

38. See also Hurowitz 2006: 15–17.

39. Wiggermann 1996.

40. Wiggermann 1992: 19; and on *Lamashtu*, in particular, see also Farber 1987, 2007; Tourtet 2010.

41. Comparable strictures apply to the production of magical composites on Egyptian funerary papyri, in connection with spells protecting the corpse against physical and moral degeneration (see Lucarelli 2006, 2010). Incantations in a Ptolemaic "Book of the Dead" include the instruction that they should be recited: "over a snake with two legs, a sun-disc and two horns; over two Sacred Eyes, each with two legs and wings" (Faulkner 1994: 125, ch. 163); and in another case: "over (a figurine of) Mut having three heads; one being the head of Pakhet wearing plumes, a second being a human head wearing the Double Crown, the third being the head of a vulture wearing plumes. She also has a phallus, wings, and the claws of a lion." The text goes on to prescribe that the images should be: "Drawn in dried myrrh with fresh incense, repeated in ink upon a fresh bandage. A dwarf stands before her, another behind her, each facing her and wearing plumes. Each has a raised arm and two heads, one is the head of a falcon, the other a human head" (ibid., ch. 164).

42. See, more generally, Ataç 2010.

43. Porada 1995: 74.

44. See Burkert 1992: 82–87.

45. Napier 1986: 107–109.

46. For technical analysis of mold-made Gorgon-heads on Greek architectural terracottas, see N. A. Winter 1993.

47. Napier 1986: 99; cf. Mack 2002: 576–578.

48. Herrmann and Millard 2003.

49. Ataç 2004.

50. See also Radner 2009.

51. For the immunological paradigm in modern cultures of governance, and its demonological origins, see Napier 2003.

CONCLUSION

1. Wittkower 1942.

2. See also Lenfant 1995.

3. Friedman 2000: 132.

4. See Mitter 1992.

5. Wittkower 1942: 197.

6. Scott 1998.

7. Tomasello 1999: 204.

REFERENCES

Akkermans, P.M.M.G., and G. M. Schwartz. 2003. *The Archaeology of Syria: From Complex Hunter-Gatherers to Early Urban Societies (c. 16,000–300 BC)*. Cambridge, UK: Cambridge University Press.

Algaze, G. 1993. *The Uruk World System: The Dynamics of Expansion of Early Mesopotamian Civilization*. Chicago: Chicago University Press.

Al-Sindī, K. M. 1999. *Dilmun Seals. Part 1*, trans. M. A. Al-Khozai. Bahrain: Ministry of Cabinet Affairs and Information, Bahrain National Museum.

Altenmüller, H. 1965. *Die Apotropaia und die Götter Mittelägyptens*. 2 volumes. PhD dissertation, Ludwig-Maximilian-Universität zu München.

———. 1983. Ein Zaubermesser aus Tübingen. *Die Welt des Orients* 14: 30–54.

———. 1986. Ein Zaubermesser des Mittleren Reiches. *Studien zue altägyptischen Kultur* 13: 1–27.

Amiet, P. 1966. *Elam*. Auvers-sur-Oise: Archée.

———. 1972. *Glyptique susienne: des origins à l'époque des Perses Achéménides*. Paris: Geuthner.

———. 1980. *La glyptique Mésopotamienne archaïque*. Paris: CNRS.

———. 1986. *L'âge des échanges inter-iranien 3500–1700 avant J.-C*. Notes et documents des musées de France XI. Paris: Éditions de la Réunion des musées nationaux.

Andriolo, K. R. 1979. *Kulturkreislehre* and the Austrian mind. *Man* (N.S.) 14 (1): 133–144.

Arnheim, R. 1966 [1949]. A note on monsters. In *Towards a Psychology of Art*, ed. R. Arnheim, pp. 255–257. London: Faber.

Aruz, J. 1999. Images of the supernatural world: Bactria-Margiana seals and relations with the Near East and the Indus. *Ancient Civilizations from Scythia to Siberia* 5: 12–30.

———, ed. 2003a. *Art of the First Cities: The Third Millennium B.C. from the Mediterranean to the Indus*. New York: Metropolitan Museum of Art.

———. 2003b. "Intercultural style" carved chlorite objects. In Aruz, ed. (2003a), pp. 325–346.

Aruz, J. 2008a. *Marks of Distinction: Seals and Cultural Exchange between the Aegean and the Orient* (ca. 2600–1360 BC). Corpus der Minoischen und Mykenischen Siegel 7. Mainz am Rhein: Philipp von Zabern.

———. 2008b. Ritual and royal imagery. In *Beyond Babylon: Art, Trade, and Diplomacy in the Second Millennium BC*, ed. J. Aruz, K. Benzel, and J. M. Evans, pp. 136–150. New York: Metropolitan Museum of Art; New Haven, CT, and London: Yale University Press.

Aruz, J., A. Farkas, A. Alekseev, and E. Korolkova, eds. 2000. *The Golden Deer of Eurasia: Scythian and Sarmatian Treasures from the Russian Steppes*. New York: Metropolitan Museum of Art.

Aruz, J., A. Farkas, and E. V. Fino, eds. 2006. *The Golden Deer of Eurasia: Perspectives on the Steppe Nomads of the Ancient World*. New York: Metropolitan Museum of Art.

Asma, S. T. 2009. *On Monsters: An Unnatural History of Our Worst Fears*. New York and London: Oxford University Press.

Asselberghs, H. 1961. *Chaos en Beheersing: documenten uit aeneolithisch Egypte*. Leiden: E. J. Brill.

Ataç, M.-A. 2004. The "underworld vision" of the Ninivite intellectual milieu. *Iraq* 66: 67–76.

———. 2010. *The Mythology of Kingship in Neo-Assyrian Art*. Cambridge, UK: Cambridge University Press.

Atran, S. 1990. *Cognitive Foundations of Natural History: Towards an Anthropology of Science*. Cambridge, UK: Cambridge University Press.

———. 2002. *In Gods We Trust: The Evolutionary Landscape of Religion*. Oxford, UK: Oxford University Press.

Atran, S., and D. Medin. 2008. *The Native Mind and the Cultural Construction of Nature*. Cambridge, MA, and London: MIT Press.

Auerbach, E. 1994. *Terracotta Plaques from the Diyala and Their Archaeological and Cultural Contexts*. Chicago: University of Chicago, UMI Dissertation Services.

Auger, E. E. 2005. *The Way of Inuit Art: Aesthetics and History in and beyond the Arctic*. London: McFarland.

el-Baghdadi, S. G. 1999. La palette décorée de Minshat Ezzat (Delta). *Archéo-Nil* 9: 9–11.

Bagley, R. W. 1987. *Shang Ritual Bronzes in the Arthur M. Sackler Collections*. Cambridge, MA: Harvard University Press.

———. 1990. Shang ritual bronzes: casting technique and vessel design. *Archives of Asian Art* 43: 6–20.

———. 1993. Replication techniques in Eastern Zhou bronze casting. In *History from Things: Essays on Material Culture*, ed. S. Lubar and W. D. Kingery, pp. 231–241. Washington, DC, and London: Smithsonian Institution Press.

————. 1996. Debris from the Houma foundry. *Orientations* 27 (9): 50–58.

————. 2006. Ornament, representation, and imaginary animals in Bronze Age China. *Arts Asiatiques* 61: 17–29.

————. 2008. *Max Loehr and the Study of Chinese Bronzes: Style and Classification in the History of Art*. Ithaca, NY: East Asia Program, Cornell University.

————. 2009. Anyang mold-making and the decorated model. *Artibus Asiae* 69 (1): 39–90.

Bahn, P. 1997. Membrane and numb brain: a close look at a recent claim for shamanism in Palaeolithic art. *Rock Art Research* 14: 62–68.

Bahn, P., and J. Vertut. 1988. *Images of the Ice Age*. Leicester, UK: Windward.

Baines, J. 1995. Origins of Egyptian kingship. In *Ancient Egyptian Kingship*, ed. D. O'Connor and D. P. Silverman, pp. 95–156. Leiden, New York, and Köln: E. J. Brill.

————. 2007. *Visual and Written Culture in Ancient Egypt*. Oxford, UK: Oxford University Press.

Barber, E.J.W. 1991. *Prehistoric Textiles: The Development of Cloth in the Neolithic and Bronze Ages with Special Reference to the Aegean*. Princeton, NJ: Princeton University Press.

Barrett, H. C., and R. Kurzban. 2006. Modularity in cognition: framing the debate. *Psychological Review* 113 (3): 628–647.

Barrett, J. L. 2004. *Why Would Anyone Believe in God?* Walnut Creek, CA: Altamira Press.

Barth, F. 1990. The Guru and the Conjurer: transactions in knowledge and the shaping of culture in Southeast Asia and Melanesia. *Man* 25: 640–653.

Bateson, G. 1972. *Steps to an Ecology of Mind: Collected Essays in Anthropology, Psychiatry, Evolution, and Epistemology*. Chicago: University of Chicago Press.

Baumgartel, E. J. 1960. *Cultures of Prehistoric Egypt* II. London: Oxford University Press for Griffith Institute.

Baxandall, M. 1972. *Painting and Experience in Fifteenth Century Italy: A Primer in the Social History of Pictorial Style*, 2nd ed. Oxford, UK: Oxford University Press.

Bellwood, P. 2005. *The First Farmers: The Origins of Agricultural Societies*. Malden, MA, and Oxford, UK: Blackwell.

Belting, H. 2005. Image, medium, body: a new approach to iconology. *Critical Inquiry* 31: 302–319.

Benedict, R. 1935. *Patterns of Culture*. London: Routledge.

Benjamin, W. 1999 [1936]. *Illuminations*. London: Pimlico.

Berlin, B. 1992. *Ethnobiological Classification: Principles of Categorization of Plants and Animals in Traditional Societies*. Princeton, NJ: Princeton University Press.

Bevan, A. 2007. *Stone Vessels and Values in the Bronze Age Mediterranean*. Cambridge, UK: Cambridge University Press.

Bildhauer, B., and R. Mills, eds. 2003. *The Monstrous Middle Ages*. Cardiff, UK: University of Wales Press.

Black, J., and A. Green. 1992. *Gods, Demons and Symbols of Ancient Mesopotamia: An Illustrated Dictionary*. London: British Museum Press.

Bleek, W.H.I., and L. C. Lloyd. 1911. *Specimens of Bushman Folklore*. London: Allen and Co.

Bloch, M. 2005. *Essays on Cultural Transmission*. Oxford and New York: Berg.

Boardman, J. 2002. *The Archaeology of Nostalgia*. London: Thames and Hudson.

Boehmer, R. M. 1974a. Das Rollsiegel im prädynastischen Ägypten. *Archäologischer Anzeiger* 4: 495–514.

———. 1974b. Orientalische Einflüsse auf verzierten Messergriffen aus dem prädynastichen Ägypten. *Archäologischen Mitteilungen aus Iran* 7: 15–40.

Bonnet, C. 2000. *Edifices et rites funéraires à Kerma*. Paris: Errance.

Borić, D. 2007. Images of animality: hybrid bodies and mimesis in early prehistoric art. In *Image and Imagination: A Global Prehistory of Figurative Representation*, ed. C. Renfrew and I. Morley, pp. 83–101. Cambridge, UK: McDonald Institute.

Bowersock, G. W. 1974. "The social and economic history of the Roman Empire" by Michael Ivanovitch Rostovtzeff. *Daedalus* 103 (1): 15–23.

Boyd, B. 2009. *On the Origin of Stories: Evolution, Cognition, and Fiction*. Cambridge, MA: Belknap Press of Harvard University Press.

Boyer, P., ed. 1992. *Cognitive Aspects of Religious Symbolism*. New York: Cambridge University Press.

———. 1994. *The Naturalness of Religious Ideas: A Cognitive Theory of Religion*. Berkeley, CA, and London: University of California Press.

———. 2000. Functional origins of religious concepts: ontological and strategic selection in evolved minds. *Journal of the Royal Anthropological Institute* 6 (2): 195–214.

———. 2001. *Religion Explained*. London: Heinemann.

Boyer, P., and C. Ramble. 2001. Cognitive templates for religious concepts: cross-cultural evidence for recall of counter-intuitive representations. *Cognitive Science* 25: 535–564.

Brandes, M. 1979. *Siegelabrollungen aus den archäischen Bauschichten in Uruk-Warka*. Wiesbaden: Franz Steiner.

———. 1986. Commemorative seals? In *Insight through Images: Studies in Honor of Edith Porada*, ed. M. Kelly-Buccellati, pp. 51–56. Malibu, CA: Undena.

Breniquet, C. 1992. A propos du vase Halafien de la tombe G2 de Tell Arpachiya. *Iraq* 54: 69–78.

Breuil, H. 1952. *Four Hundred Centuries of Cave Art*, trans. M. E. Boyle. Montignac and Paris: Centre d'Études et de Documentation Préhistoriques.

Burkert, W. 1992. *The Orientalizing Revolution: Near Eastern Influence on Greek Culture in the Early Archaic Age*. Cambridge, MA: Harvard University Press.

Bussmann, R. 2010. *Die Provinztempel Ägyptens von der 0. bis zur 11. Dynastie: Archäologie und Geschichte einer gesellschaftlichen Institution zwischen Residenz und Provinz*. Leiden: Brill.

Caldwell, D. H. 1976. The early glyptic of Gawra, Giyan, and Susa and the development of long-distance trade. *Orientalia* 45: 227–250.

Canetti, E. 2000 [1960]. *Crowds and Power*. New York: Farrar, Straus, and Giroux.

Carey, S. 1985. *Conceptual Change in Childhood*. Cambridge,MA, and London: MIT Press.

Carey, S., and E. S. Spelke. 1994. Domain-specific knowledge and conceptual change. In *Mapping the Mind: Domain Specificity in Cognition and Culture*, ed. L. A. Hirschfeld and S. A. Gelman, pp. 169–200. Cambridge, UK: Cambridge University Press.

Carter, J. 1987. The masks of Ortheia. *American Journal of Archaeology* 91 (3): 355–383.

Case, H., and J. C. Payne. 1962. Tomb 100: the decorated tomb at Hierakonpolis. *Journal of Egyptian Archaeology* 48: 5–18.

Cauvin, J. 1994. *Naissance des divinités, naissance de l'agriculture. La Révolution des symboles au Néolithique*. Paris: C.N.R.S. Éditions.

———. 2000. *The Birth of the Gods and the Origins of Agriculture*, trans. T. Watkins. Cambridge, UK: Cambridge University Press.

Chang, K. C. 1963. The animal in Shang and Chou bronze art. *Bulletin of the Institute of Ethnology, Academia Sinica* 16: 527–554.

———. 1983. *Art, Myth, and Ritual: The Path to Political Authority in Ancient China*. Cambridge, MA, and London: Harvard University Press.

———. 1999. China on the eve of the Historical Period. In *The Cambridge History of Ancient China*, ed. M. Loewe and E. L. Shaughnessy, pp. 37–73. Cambridge, UK: Cambridge University Press.

Charvát, P. 2002. *Mesopotamia before History*. London: Routledge.

Cherry, J. 2010. Sorting out Crete's prepalatial off-island interactions. In W.A. Parkinson and M. L. Galaty, eds. (2010), pp. 107–140.

Childe, V. G. 1936. *Man Makes Himself*. London: Watts and Co.

Churcher, C. S. 1984. Zoological study of the ivory knife handle from Abu Zaidan. In Needler (1984), pp. 152–169.

Ciałowicz, K. M. 1991. *Les palettes égyptiennes aux motifs zoomorphes et sans décoration: études de l'art prédynastique*. Kraków: Uniwersytet Jagielloński.

———. 2007. *Ivory and Gold: Beginnings of the Egyptian Art*. Poznan: Poznan Prehistoric Society.

Clark, A. 1997. *Being There: Putting Brain, Body, and World Together Again*. Cambridge, MA: MIT Press.

Clottes, J., and J. D. Lewis-Williams. 1998. *The Shamans of Prehistory: Trance and Magic in the Painted Caves*, trans. S. Hawkes. New York: Harry N. Abrams.

Cohen, J. J., ed. 1996. *Monster Theory: Reading Culture*. Minneapolis and London: University of Minnesota Press.

Cohen, R., and R. Westbrook. 2000. *Amarna Diplomacy: The Beginnings of International Relations*. Baltimore and London: Johns Hopkins University Press.

Collon, D. 2005. *First Impressions: Cylinder Seals in the Ancient Near East*. London: British Museum.

Conard, N. J. 2003. Palaeolithic ivory sculptures from southwestern Germany and the origins of figurative art. *Nature* 426: 830–832.

Conkey, M. W., O. Soffer, D. Stratmann, and N. G. Jablonski. 1997. *Beyond Art: Pleistocene Image and Symbol*. San Francisco: California Academy of Sciences.

Cool Root, M., ed. 2005. *This Fertile Land: Signs and Symbols in the Early Arts of Iran and Iraq*. Ann Arbor, IL: Kelsey Museum of Archaeology.

Crawford, H. 1998. *Dilmun and Its Gulf Neighbours*. Cambridge, UK: Cambridge University Press.

Crowley, J. L. 1989. *The Aegean and the East: An Investigation into the Transference of Artistic Motifs between the Aegean, Egypt, and the Near East in the Bronze Age*. Jonsered, Sweden: Paul Åströms.

———. 2008. Mycenaean art and architecture. In *The Cambridge Companion to the Aegean Bronze Age*, ed. C. W. Shelmerdine, pp. 258–288. New York: Cambridge University Press.

Davidoff, J., and D. Roberson. 2002. Development of animal recognition: a difference between parts and wholes. *Journal of Experimental Child Psychology* 81: 217–34.

de Beaune, S. 1998. Chamanisme et préhistoire: un feuilleton à épisodes. *L'Homme* 147: 203–219.

Dehaene, S. 1997. *The Number Sense: How the Mind Creates Mathematics*. Oxford, UK: Oxford University Press.

de Miroschedji, P. 1973. Vases et objets en stéatite susiens du Musée du Louvre. *Cahiers de la Délégation Archéologique Française en Iran* 3: 9–79.

Descola, P. 1996. Constructing natures: symbolic ecology and social practice. In *Nature and Society: Anthropological Perspectives*, ed. P. Descola
and G. Pálsson, pp. 82–102. London: Routledge.

———. 2005. Beyond nature and culture. *Proceedings of the British Academy*
139: 137–155.

———, ed. 2010. *La fabrique des images: visions du monde et forms de la representation*. Paris: Somogy/Éditions d'Art.

Dickinson. O.T.P.K. 1994. *The Aegean Bronze Age*. Cambridge, UK: Cambridge University Press.

Di Cosmo, N. 1999. The northern frontier in Pre-Imperial China. In *The
Cambridge History of Ancient China*, ed. M. Loewe and E. L. Shaughnessy, pp. 858–966. Cambridge, UK: Cambridge University Press.

Dittmann, R. 1986. Seals, sealings, and tablets: thoughts on the chang-
ing pattern of administrative control from the Late-Uruk to the
Proto-Elamite period at Susa. In *Gamdat Nasr: Period or Regional
Style?*, ed. U. Finkbeiner and W. Röllig, pp. 332–366. Wiesbaden:
Reichert.

Dreyer, G., R. Hartmann, U. Hartung, T. Hikade, H. Köpp, C. Lacher,
V. Müller, A. Nerlich, and A. Zink. 2003. Umm el-Qaab: Nachunt-
ersuchungen im frühzeitlichen Königsfriedhof. 13./14./15. Vorb-
ericht. *Mitteilungen des Deutschen Archäologischen Instituts, Abteilung
Kairo* 59: 67–138.

Dubiel, U. 2008. *Amulette, Siegel und Perlen: Studien zu Typologie und Tragesitte
im Alten und Mittleren Reich*. Fribourg: Academic Press; Göttingen:
Vandenhoeck and Ruprecht.

Eckmann, C., and Shafik, S. 2005. *Leben dem Horus Pepi: Restaurierung und
technologische Untersuchung der Metallskulpturen des Pharao Pepi I. aus
Hierakonpolis*. Mainz: Verlag des Römisch-Germanischen Zentral-
museums.

Eisenstein, E. L. 1983. *The Printing Revolution in Early Modern Europe*. Cambridge, UK: Cambridge University Press.

Eliade, M. 1964. *Shamanism: Archaic Techniques of Ecstasy*. Princeton, NJ:
Princeton University Press.

Elsner, J. 2006. From empirical evidence to the big picture: some reflections
on Riegl's concept of *Kunstwollen*. *Critical Inquiry* 32: 741–766.

Emery, W. B. 1961. *Archaic Egypt*. Harmondsworth, UK: Penguin.

Englund, R. K. 1998. Texts from the Late Uruk period. In *Mesopotamien:
Späturuk-Zeit und Frühdynastiche Zeit, Annäherungen 1*, ed. P. Attinger
and M. Wäffler, pp. 15–233. Fribourg: Universitätsverlag.

Falkenhausen, L. von. 2004. Review of Puett 2002. *Harvard Journal of Asiatic
Studies* 64 (3): 465–479.

Falkenhausen, L. von. 2006. *Chinese Society in the Age of Confucius (1000–250 BC): The Archaeological Evidence*. Los Angeles: University of California, Cotsen Institute of Archaeology.

Farber, W. 1987. Tamarisken-Fibeln-Skolopender. Zur philologischen Deutung der "Reiseszene" auf neo-assyrischen Lamaštu-Amuletten. *American Oriental Series* 67: 85–105.

———. 2007. Lamaštu—agent of a specific disease or a generic destroyer of health? In *Disease in Babylonia*, ed. I. Finkel and M. Geller, pp. 137–145. Leiden: Brill.

Farkas, A. E., P. O. Harper, and E. B. Harrison, eds. 1987. *Monsters and Demons in the Ancient and Medieval Worlds: Papers Presented in Honor of Edith Porada*. Mainz on Rhine: Philipp von Zabern.

Faulkner, R. O. 1994. *The Egyptian Book of the Dead*. San Francisco: Chronicle Books.

Feldman, M. 2002. Luxurious forms: redefining a Mediterranean "international style," 1400–1200 B.C.E. *The Art Bulletin* 84 (1): 6–29.

———. 2006. *Diplomacy by Design: Luxury Arts and an "International Style" in the Ancient Near East, 1400–1200 BCE*. Chicago: Chicago University Press.

Fischer, H. G. 1958. A fragment of a late predynastic Egyptian relief from the Eastern Delta. *Artibus Asiae* 21: 64–88.

———. 1978. The evolution of composite hieroglyphs in ancient Egypt. *Metropolitan Museum Journal* 12: 5–19.

———. 1987. The ancient Egyptian attitude towards the monstrous. In A. E. Farkas et al., eds. (1987), pp. 13–26.

Flores, D. V. 2003. *Funerary Sacrifice of Animals in the Egyptian Predynastic Period*. Oxford, UK: British Archaeological Reports.

Francfort, H.-P. 1994. The Central Asian dimension of the symbolic system in Bactria and Margiana. *Antiquity* 68: 406–418.

Frankfort, H. 1932. The Indus civilization and the Near East. *Annual Bibliography of Indian Archaeology* 7: 1–12.

———. 1935. *Oriental Institute Discoveries in Iraq, 1933/34: Fourth Preliminary Report of the Iraq Expedition*. Oriental Institute Communications 19. Chicago: University of Chicago Press.

———. 1936. Notes on the Cretan griffin. *Annual of the British School at Athens* 37: 106–122.

———. 1939. *Cylinder Seals: A Documentary Essay on the Art and Religion of the Ancient Near East*. London: Macmillan.

———. 1941. The origin of monumental architecture in Egypt. *American Journal of Semitic Languages and Literatures* 58: 329–358.

———. 1948. *Ancient Egyptian Religion: An Interpretation*. New York: Columbia University Press.

———. 1951. *The Birth of Civilization in the Near East*. Bloomington: Indiana University Press.

———. 1996. *The Art and Architecture of the Ancient Orient*, 5th ed., with supplementary notes and additional bibliography and abbreviations by M. Roaf and D. Matthews. New Haven, CT, and London: Yale University Press.

Friedman, J. B. 2000. *The Monstrous Races in Medieval Art and Thought*. Syracuse, NY: Syracuse University Press.

Friedman, R. F. 1996. The ceremonial centre at Hierakonpolis Locality HK29A. In *Aspects of Early Egypt*, ed. A. J. Spencer, pp. 16–35. London: British Museum.

———. 2008. Excavating Egypt's early kings: recent discoveries in the elite cemetery at Hierakonpolis. In *Egypt at Its Origins, 2: Proceedings of the International Conference "Origin of the State, Predynastic and Early Dynastic Egypt," Toulouse, France, 5th–8th September 2005*, ed. B. Midant-Reynes and Y. Tristant, pp. 1157–1195. Leuven: Peeters.

Gale, R., P. Gasson, N. Hepper, and G. Killen. 2000. Furniture. In *Ancient Egyptian Materials and Technology*, ed. P. T. Nicholson and I. Shaw, pp. 334–371. Cambridge, UK: Cambridge University Press.

Gell, A. 1998. *Art and Agency: An Anthropological Theory*. Oxford, UK: Oxford University Press.

Geupel, V. 1977. Das Rötelgrab von Bad Dürrenberg, Kr. Merseburg. In *Archäologie als Geschichtswissenschaft. Schriften zur Ur- und Frügeschichte* 30, ed. J. Herrmann, pp. 101–110. Berlin: VEB Deutscher Verlag der Wissenschaften.

Gifford-Gonzalez, D. 2007. On beasts in breasts: another reading of women, wildness and danger at Çatalhöyük. *Archaeological Dialogues* 14: 91–111.

Goetze, A. 1970. Early Dynastic dedication inscriptions from Nippur. *Journal of Cuneiform Studies* 23 (2): 39–56.

Goff, B. 1963. *Symbols of Prehistoric Mesopotamia*. New Haven, CT, and London: Yale University Press.

Gombrich, E. H. 1984. *The Sense of Order: A Study in the Psychology of Decorative Art*, 2nd ed. Oxford, UK: Phaidon.

———. 1988. *The Uses of Images: Studies in the Social Function of Art and Visual Communication*. London: Phaidon.

Goring-Morris, N., and L. Kolska Horwitz. 2007. Funerals and feasts during the Pre–Pottery Neolithic B of the Near East. *Antiquity* 81: 902–919.

Graf, F. 1999. Mythical production: mythical responses to technology in antiquity. In *From Myth to Reason: Studies in the Development of Greek Thought*, ed. R. Buxton, pp. 317–328. Oxford, UK: Oxford University Press.

Green, A. 1983. Neo-Assyrian apotropaic figures: figurines, rituals and mon- umental art, with special reference to the figurines from the excava- tions of the British School of Archaeology in Iraq at Nimrud. *Iraq* 45 (1): 87–96.

——. 1994. Mischwesen. B. In *Reallexikon der Assyriologie und Vorder- asiatischen Archäologie* 8, ed. E. Ebeling and B. Meissner, pp. 246– 264. Berlin: de Gruyter.

Grosman, L., N. D. Munro, and A. Belfer-Cohen. 2008. A 12,000-year-old shaman burial from the southern Levant (Israel). *Proceedings of the National Academy of Sciences of the United States of America* 105 (46): 17665–17669.

Guenther, M. 1999. *Tricksters and Trancers: Bushman Religion and Society.* Bloomington and Indianapolis: Indiana University Press.

Gundlach, R. 1986. Thoeris. *Lexikon der Ägyptologie* 6, ed. W. Helck and E. Otto, pp. 494–497. Wiesbaden: Harrassowitz.

Gunter, A. C. 2009. *Greek Art and the Orient.* Cambridge, UK: Cambridge University Press.

Gurney, O. R. 1935. Babylonian prophylactic figures and their rituals. *An- nals of Archaeology and Anthropology* 22: 31–96.

Guthrie, R. D. 2005. *The Nature of Paleolithic Art.* Chicago and London: Uni- versity of Chicago Press.

Hahn, J. 1986. *Kraft und Aggression: Die Botschaft der Eiszeitkunst im Aurigna- cien?* Tübingen: Archaeologica Venatoria.

Hallager, E., and Weingarten, J. 1993. The five roundels from Malia, with a note on two new Minoan Genii. *Bulletin de Correspondence Hellé- nique* 117: 1–18.

Hallowell, A. I. 1955. The recapitulation theory and culture. In A. Irving Hallowell, *Culture and Experience*, pp. 32–74 (originally published as The child, the savage and human experience, *Proceedings of the Sixth Institute on the Exceptional Child*, 1939). Philadelphia: Univer- sity of Pennsylvania Press.

Helmer, D., L. Gourichon, and D. Stordeur. 2004. A l'Aube de la Domestica- tion Animale. Imaginaire et Symbolisme Animal dans les Premières Sociétés Néolithiques du Nord du Proche-Orient. *Anthropozoologica* 39: 143–163.

Hendrickx, S. 1998. Peaux d'animaux comme symboles prédynastiques. A propos de quelques representations sur les vases *White Cross-Lined*. *Chronique d'Egypte* 73: 203–230.

Hendrickx, S., and P. Vermeersch. 2000. Prehistory: from the Palaeolithic to the Badarian culture. In *The Oxford History of Ancient Egypt*, ed. I. Shaw, pp. 17–44. Oxford, UK: Oxford University Press.

Herles, M. 2006. *Götterdarstellungen Mesopotamiens in der 2. Hälfte des 2. Jahrtausends v. Chr.: Das Anthropomorphe Bild im Verhältnis zum Symbol.* Münster: Ugarit–Verlag.

Herrmann, G., and A. Millard. 1993. Who used ivories in the early first millennium BC? In *Culture through Objects: Ancient Near Eastern Studies in Honour of P.R.S. Moorey*, ed. T. F. Potts, M. Roaf, and D. Stein, pp. 377–402. Oxford, UK: Griffith Institute.

Hill, M. 2007. *Gifts for the Gods: Images from Egyptian Temples.* New Haven, CT, and London: Yale University Press.

Hirschfeld, L. A., and S. A. Gelman, eds. 1994. *Mapping the Mind: Domain Specificity in Cognition and Culture.* Cambridge, UK: Cambridge University Press.

Hodder, I. 2006. *Çatalhöyük: The Leopard's Tale: Revealing the Mysteries of Turkey's Ancient "Town."* London: Thames and Hudson.

———, ed. 2010. *Religion in the Emergence of Civilization: Çatalhöyük as a Case Study.* Cambridge, UK, and New York: Cambridge University Press.

———. 2011. Wheels of time: some aspects of entanglement theory and the Secondary Products Revolution. *Journal of World Prehistory* 24: 175–187.

Hodder, I., and L. M. Meskell. 2010. The symbolism of Çatalhöyük in its regional context. In I. Hodder, ed. (2010), pp. 32–72.

Hoffman, M. A., B. Adams, M. Berger, M. N. el-Hadidi, J. F. Harlan, H. A. Hamroush, C. Lupton, J. McArdle, W. McHugh, R. O. Allen, and M. Rogers. 1982. *The Predynastic of Hierakonpolis—An Interim Report.* Giza: Cairo University Herbarium; Department of Sociology and Anthropology, Western Illinois University.

Hopkins, C. 1934. Assyrian elements in the Perseus-Gorgon story. *American Journal of Archaeology* 38: 341–358.

———. 1961. The sunny side of the Greek gorgon. *Berytus* 14: 25–35.

Hornung, E. 1982. *Conceptions of God in Ancient Egypt: The One and the Many*, trans. J. Baines. Ithaca, NY: Cornell University Press.

———. 2000. Komposite Gottheiten in der ägyptischen Ikonographie. In *Images as Media: Sources for the Cultural History of the Near East and Eastern Mediterranean (1st millennium BCE)*, ed. C. Uehlinger, pp. 1–20. Freiburg: University Press; Göttingen: Vandenhoeck and Ruprecht.

Houston, S. D., ed. 2004. *The First Writing: Script Invention as History and Process.* Cambridge, UK: Cambridge University Press.

Hurowitz, V. 2006. What goes in is what comes out: materials for creating cult statues. In *Text, Artifact, and Image: Revealing Ancient Israelite Religion*, ed. G. M. Beckman and T. J. Lewis, pp. 3–23. Providence, RI: Brown Judaic Studies.

Hutton, R. 2001. *Shamans: Siberian Spirituality and the Western Imagination.* London and New York: Hambledon and London.

Huyge, D. 2004. A double-powerful device for regeneration: the Abu Zaidan knife handle reconsidered. In *Egypt at Its Origins: Studies in Memory of Barbara Adams,* ed. S. Hendrickx, R. F. Friedman, K. M. Ciałowicz, and M. Chłodnicki, pp. 823–836. Leuven: Peeters.

Immerwahr, S. A. 1990. *Aegean Painting in the Bronze Age.* University Park, PA, and London: Pennsylvania State University Press.

Ingold, T. 2000. Totemism, animism and the depiction of animals. In T. Ingold, *The Perception of the Environment,* pp. 111–131. London: Routledge.

Iversen, M. 1993. *Alois Riegl: Art History and Theory.* Cambridge, MA: MIT Press.

Jasim, S. A., and J. Oates. 1986. Early tokens and tablets in Mesopotamia: new information from Tell Abada and Tell Brak. *World Archaeology* 17: 348–361.

Jolly, P. 2002. Therianthropes in San rock art. *South African Archaeological Bulletin* 57 (176): 85–103.

Johnson, K. 2005. Modes of religious experience in late prehistory. In Cool Root, ed. (2005), pp. 73–86.

Johnston, A. 1993. Pre-classical Greece. In *The Oxford History of Classical Art,* ed. John Boardman, pp. 11–82. Oxford, UK: Oxford University Press.

Kaiser, W. 1990. Zur Entstehung des gesamtägyptischen Staates. *Mitteilungen des Deutschen Archäologischen Instituts, Abteilung Kairo* 46: 287–299.

Kantor, H. J. 1956. Syro-Palestinian ivories. *Journal of Near Eastern Studies* 15 (3): 153–174.

———. 1962. A bronze plaque with relief decoration from Tell Tainat. *Journal of Near Eastern Studies* 21: 93–117.

———. 1992. The relative chronology of Egypt and its foreign correlations before the First Intermediate Period. In *Chronologies in Old World Archaeology,* 3rd ed., 2 volumes, ed. R. W. Ehrich, pp. 3–21. Chicago and London: University of Chicago Press.

———. 1997 [1947]. *The Aegean and the Orient in the Second Millennium BC.* Archaeological Institute of America Monograph, no.1. Reprint, Boston: Archaeological Institute of America.

Kanwisher, N., J. McDermott, and M. M. Chun. 1997. The fusiform face area: a module in human extrastriate cortex specialized for face perception. *Journal of Neuroscience* 17: 4302–4311.

Karadimas, D. 2010. Animaux imaginaires et êtres composites. In *La fabrique des images: visions du monde et forms de la representation,* ed. P. Descola, pp. 185–192. Paris: Somogy/Éditions d'Art.

Karageorghis, V. 1993. *The Coroplastic Art of Ancient Cyprus*. Nicosis: A. G. Leventis Foundation.

Karetsou, A., ed. 2001. *Kriti-Egyptos. Politismikoi Desmoi Trion Khilietion*. Athens: Kapon.

Karo, G. 1930. *Die Schachtgräber von Mykenai*. 2 volumes. Munich: Bruckmann.

Keightley, D. N. 1998. Shamanism, death and the ancestors: religious mediation in Neolithic and Shang China (ca. 5000–1000 BC). *Asiatische Studien* 52 (3): 763–831.

Kemp, B. J., and R. S. Merrillees. 1980. *Minoan Pottery in Second Millennium Egypt*. Mainz am Rhein: Philipp von Zabern.

Kendall, T. 1997. *Kerma and the Kingdom of Kush, 2500–1500 B.C.: The Archaeological Discovery of an Ancient Nubian Empire*. Washington, DC: National Museum of African Art, Smithsonian Institution.

Kenoyer, J. M. 1998. *Ancient Cities of the Indus Valley Civilization*. Karachi and Oxford, UK: Oxford University Press.

Kesner, L. 1991. The *taotie* reconsidered: meanings and functions of the Shang theriomorphic imagery. *Artibus Asiae* 51 (1/2): 29–53.

Killen, G. 1980. *Ancient Egyptian Furniture* I: *4000–1300 BC*. Warminster: Aris & Phillips.

Klengel-Brandt, E. 1968. Apotropäische Tonfiguren aus Assur. *Forschungen und Berichte* 10: 19–37.

Köcher, F. 1953. Der Babylonische Göttertypentext. *Mitteilungen des Instituts für Orientforschung* 1: 57–107.

Kohl, P. 1978. The balance of trade in southwestern Asia in the mid-third millennium BC. *Current Anthropology* 19: 463–492.

———. 2001. Reflections on the production of chlorite at Tepe Yahya: 25 years later. In *Excavations at Tepe Yahya, Iran 1967–1975*, ed. C. C. Lamberg-Karlovsky and D.T.F. Potts, pp. 209–230. American School of Prehistoric Research Bulletin 45. Harvard, MA: Peabody Museum of Archaeology and Ethnology.

———. 2007. *The Making of Bronze Age Eurasia*. Cambridge, UK: Cambridge University Press.

Kohl, P., G. Harbottle, and E. V. Sayre. 1979. Physical and chemical analyses of soft stone vessels from Southwest Asia. *Archeometry* 21: 131–159.

Kostoula, M., and J. Maran. 2012. A group of animal-headed faience vessels from Tiryns. In *All the Wisdom of the East: Studies in Near Eastern Archaeology and History in Honor of Eliezer D. Oren*, ed. M. Gruber, S. Ahituv, G. Lehmann, and Z. Talshir, pp. 193–234. Fribourg: Orbis Biblicus et Orientalis.

Kroeper, K., and L. Krzyżaniak. 1992. Two ivory boxes from Early Dynastic graves in Minshat Abu Omar. In *The Followers of Horus: Studies Dedi-*

cated to Michael Allen Hoffman, ed. R. Friedman and B. Adams, pp. 207–214. Oxford, UK: Oxbow Books.

Krzyszkowska, O. 2005. *Aegean Seals: An Introduction*. London: Institute of Classical Studies.

Küchler, S. 2002. *Malanggan: Art, Memory, and Sacrifice*. Oxford, UK, and New York: Berg.

———. 2005. Materiality and cognition: the changing face of things. In *Materiality*, ed. D. Miller, pp. 206–230. Durham, NC, and London: Duke University Press.

Lamberg-Karlovsky, C. C. 1988. The "Inter-Cultural Style" carved vessels. *Iranica Antiqua* 23: 45–95.

Lambrou-Phillipson, C. 1990. *Hellenorientalia: The Near Eastern Presence in the Bronze Age Aegean, ca. 3000–1100 B.C.; plus, Orientalia: A Catalogue of Egyptian, Mesopotamian, Mitannian, Syro-Palestinian, Cypriot and Asia Minor Objects from the Bronze Age Aegean*. Göteborg: Paul Åströms.

———. 1991. Seafaring in the Bronze Age Mediterranean: the parameters involved in maritime travel. In *Thalassa: L'Égée préhistorique et la mer*, ed. R. Laffineur, pp. 11–21. Aegaeum 7. Liège: Université de Liège.

Latour, B. 1987. *Science in Action: How to Follow Scientists and Engineers through Society*. Cambridge, MA: Harvard University Press.

Layton, R. 2000. Shamanism, totemism and rock art: *Les Chamanes de la Préhistoire* in the context of rock art research. *Cambridge Archaeological Journal* 10: 169–186.

Ledderose, L. 2000. *Ten Thousand Things: Module and Mass Production in Chinese Art*. Princeton, NJ: Princeton University Press.

Leevers, H. J., and P. L. Harris. 1998. Drawing impossible entities: a measure of the imagination in children with autism, children with learning disabilities, and normal 4-year-olds. *Journal of Child Psychology and Psychiatry* 39 (3): 399–410.

Lenfant, D. 1995. L'Inde de Ctésias des sources aux representations. *Topoi* 5: 309–336.

———. 1999. Monsters in Greek ethnography and society in the fifth and fourth centuries BCE. In *From Myth to Reason: Studies in the Development of Greek Thought*, ed. R. Buxton, pp. 197–214. Oxford, UK: Oxford University Press.

Leroi-Gourhan, A. 1977. Le préhistorien et le chamane. *L'Ethnographie* 74–75: 19–25.

———. 1993 [1964]. *Gesture and Speech*. Cambridge, MA: MIT Press.

Lévi-Strauss, C. 1982. *The Way of the Masks*, trans. S. Modelski. Seattle: University of Washington Press.

Lewis-Williams, J. D. 2002. *The Mind in the Cave*. London: Thames and Hudson.

Linseele, V., and W. van Neer. 2003. Gourmets or priests? Fauna from the predynastic temple. *Nekhen News* 15: 6–7.

Li Xiating and Liang Zhiming. 1996. *Art of the Houma Foundry*. Princeton, NJ: Princeton University Press.

Lloyd, G.E.R. 2007. *Cognitive Variations: Reflections on the Unity and Diversity of the Human Mind*. Oxford, UK: Clarendon Press.

Lommel, A. 1967. *Shamanism: The Beginnings of Art*. New York: McGraw-Hill.

Low, J., E. Goddard, and J. Melser. 2009. Generativity and imagination in autism spectrum disorder: evidence from individual differences in children's impossible entity drawings. *British Journal of Developmental Psychology* 27: 425–444.

Lucarelli, R. 2006. Demons in the *Book of the Dead*. In *Totenbuch-Forschungen: Gesammelte Beiträge des 2. Internationalen Totenbuch-Symposiums, Bonn, 25. bis 29. September 2005*, Studien zum Altägyptischen Totenbuch 11, ed. B. Backes, I. Munro, and S. Stöhr, pp. 203–212. Wiesbaden: Harrassowitz.

———. 2010. Demons (benevolent and malevolent). In *UCLA Encyclopedia of Egyptology*, ed. J. Dieleman and W. Wendrich, Los Angeles. Available at http://escholarship.ucop.edu/uc/item/1r72q9vv (accessed 03/04/2012).

Mack, R. 2002. Facing down Medusa (an aetiology of the gaze). *Art History* 25 (5): 571–604.

Madjidzadeh, Y. 2003. *Jiroft: The Earliest Oriental Civilization*. Tehran: Ministry of Culture and Islamic Guidance.

———. 2008. *Excavations at Tepe Ghabrestan, Iran*. Rome: IsIAO.

Madjidzadeh, Y., and H. Pittman. 2008. Excavations at Konar Sandal in the region of Jiroft in the Halil Basin: first preliminary report (2002–2008). *Iran* 46: 69–104.

Makkay, J. 1953. An important proof to the prehistory of shamanism: the interpretation on the masked human portrait of the case Les Trois Frères. *Alba Regia* (Székesfehérvar) 2–3: 5–10.

Mallowan, M.E.L., and J. C. Rose. 1935. Excavations at Tell Arpachiyah, 1933. *Iraq* 2: 1–178.

Margueron, J.-Cl. 2004. *Mari, métropole de l'Euphrate au IIIe et au début du IIe millénaire avant J.-C*. Paris: Picard.

Matthiae, P. 2003. Ebla and the early urbanization of Syria. In J. Aruz, ed. (2003a), pp. 165–178.

Matthiae, P., F. Pinnock, and G. S. Matthiae, eds. 1995. *Ebla: alle Origini della Civiltà Urbana: Trent'Anni di Scavi in Siria dell'Università di Roma "La Sapienza."* Milano: Electa.

Mayor, A. 2000. *The First Fossil Hunters: Paleontology in Greek and Roman Times*. Princeton, NJ, and Oxford, UK: Princeton University Press.

McAdam, E. 2003. Things fall apart, the centre cannot hold. In *Culture through Objects: Ancient Near Eastern Studies in Honour of P.R.S. Moorey*, ed. T. F. Potts, M. Roaf, and D. Stein, pp. 161–187. Oxford, UK: Griffith Institute.

McCown, T. 1937. Mugharet es-Skhul: description and excavation. In *The Stone Age of Mount Carmel*, ed. D. Garrod and D. Bate, pp. 91–107. Oxford, UK: Clarendon Press.

McDonald, A. 2000. Tall tails: the Seth animal reconsidered. In *Current Research in Egyptology 2000*, ed. A. McDonald and C. Riggs, pp. 75–81. Oxford, UK: British Archaeological Reports.

Mellink, M. J. 1987. Anatolian libation pourers and the Minoan Genius. In A. E. Farkas et al., eds. (1987), pp. 65–72.

Melion, W., and S. Küchler. 1991. Introduction: memory, cognition, and image production. In *Images of Memory: On Remembering and Representation*, ed. S. Küchler and W. Melion, pp. 1–47. Washington, DC: Smithsonian Institution Press.

Meskell, L. M. 2008. The nature of the beast: curating animals and ancestors at Çatalhöyük. *World Archaeology* 40 (3): 373–389.

Meskell, L. M., and Nakamura, C. 2009. Articulate bodies: forms and figures at Çatalhöyük. *Journal of Archaeological Method and Theory* 16 (3): 205–230.

Mesoudi, A., A. Whiten, and K. N. Laland. 2006. Towards a unified science of cultural evolution. *Behavioral and Brain Sciences* 29: 329–383.

Mithen, S. J. 1998a. A creative explosion? Theory of mind, language, and the disembodied mind of the Upper Palaeolithic. In *Creativity in Human Evolution and Prehistory*, ed. S. J. Mithen, pp. 165–191. London: Routledge.

———. 1998b. The supernatural beings of prehistory and the external storage of religious ideas. In *Cognition and Material Culture: The Archaeology of Symbolic Storage*, ed. C. Renfrew and C. Scarre, pp. 97–106. Cambridge, UK: McDonald Institute.

———. 2001. The evolution of imagination: an archaeological perspective. *SubStance* 30: 28–54.

———. 2003. *After the Ice: A Global Human History, 20,000–5000 BC*. London: Weidenfeld and Nicolson.

Mitter, P. 1992. *Much Maligned Monsters: A History of European Reactions to Indian Art*. Chicago: University of Chicago Press.

Momigliano, A. D. 1994 [1954]. M. I. Rostovtzeff. In *A.D. Momigliano: Studies on Modern Scholarship*, ed. G. W. Bowersock and T. J. Cornell, pp. 32–43. Berkeley: University of California Press.

Moorey, P.R.S. 1975. The terracotta plaques from Kish and Hursagkalama, c. 1850 to 1650 B.C. *Iraq* 37 (2): 79–99.

———. 1987. On tracking cultural transfers in prehistory: the case of Egypt and lower Mesopotamia in the fourth millennium BC. In *Centre and Periphery in the Ancient World*, ed. M. J. Rowlands, K. Kristiansen, and M. T. Larsen, pp. 36–46. Cambridge, UK: Cambridge University Press.

———. 1994. *Ancient Mesopotamian Materials and Industries: The Archaeological Evidence*. Oxford, UK: Clarendon Press.

———. 2003. *Idols of the People: Miniature Images of Clay in the Ancient Near East*. Oxford, UK: Oxford University Press.

Morgan, L. 1988. *The Miniature Wall Paintings of Thera: A Study in Aegean Culture and Iconography*. Cambridge, UK: Cambridge University Press.

Müller, W., and I. Pini, eds. *Iraklion, Archäologisches Museum. Teil 7. Die Siegelabdrücke von Kato Zakros, unter Einbeziehung von Funden aus anderen Museen, nach Vorarbeiten von N. Platon*. Corpus der Minoischen und Mykenischen Siegel II.7. Berlin: Gebr. Mann Verlag.

Nakamura, C. 2004. Dedicating magic: Neo-Assyrian apotropaic figurines and the protection of Assur. *World Archaeology* 36 (1): 11–25.

———. 2010. Magical deposits at Çatalhöyük: a matter of time and place? I. I. Hodder, ed. (2010), pp. 300–331.

Napier, A. D. 1986. *Masks, Transformation, and Paradox*. Berkeley: University of California Press.

———. 1990. *Foreign Bodies: Performance, Art, and Symbolic Anthropology*. Berkeley, CA, and Oxford, UK: University of California Press.

———. 2003. *The Age of Immunology: Conceiving a Future in an Alienating World*. Chicago and London: University of Chicago Press.

Needler, W. 1984. *Predynastic and Archaic Egypt in the Brooklyn Museum*. Brooklyn: The Brooklyn Museum.

New, J., L. Cosmides, and J. Tooby. 2007. Category-specific attention for animals reflects ancestral priorities, not expertise. *Proceedings of the National Academy of Sciences of the United States of America* 104: 16598–16603.

Newberry, P. 1893. *Beni Hasan I*. London: Kegan Paul.

———. 1895. *El Bersheh II*. London: Egypt Exploration Fund.

Nickel, L. 2006. Imperfect symmetry: re-thinking bronze casting technology in ancient China. *Artibus Asiae* 66 (1): 5–38.

Nissen, H. J. 1977. Aspects of the development of early cylinder seals. In *Seals and Sealing in the Ancient Near East*, ed. McG. Gibson and R. Biggs, pp. 15–24. Malibu. CA: Undena.

———. 2001. Cultural and political networks in the ancient Near East during the fourth and fifth millennia BC. In *Uruk Mesopotamia and Its*

Neighbours, ed. M. Rothman, pp. 149–180. Oxford, UK, and Santa Fe: James Currey/School of American Research Press.

Nissen, H. J., P. Damerow, and R. K. Englund. 1993. *Archaic Bookkeeping: Early Writing and Techniques of Economic Administration in the Ancient Near East.* Chicago: University of Chicago Press.

Oates, J. 1966. The baked clay figurines from Tell es-Sawwan. *Iraq* 28: 146–153.

———. 1978. Religion and ritual in sixth-millennium BC Mesopotamia. *World Archaeology* 10: 117–124.

Oates, J., and D. Oates. 1997. An open gate: cities of the fourth millennium BC (Tell Brak 1997). *Cambridge Archaeological Journal* 7: 287–297.

Ornan, T. 2004. Expelling demons at Nineveh: on the visibility of benevolent demons in the palaces of Nineveh. *Iraq* 66: 83–92.

Osborne, R. 1998. *Archaic and Classical Greek Art.* Oxford, UK: Oxford University Press.

Oyama, S., P. E. Griffiths, and R. D. Gray. 2001. *Cycles of Contingency: Developmental Systems and Evolution.* Cambridge, MA, and Boston: MIT Press.

Parkinson, W. A., and M. L. Galaty, eds. 2010. *Archaic State Interaction: The Eastern Mediterranean in the Bronze Age.* Santa Fe: School for Advanced Research Press.

Parpola, A. 1994. *Deciphering the Indus Script.* Cambridge, UK: Cambridge University Press.

———. 2011. The Harappan unicorn in Eurasian and South Asian perspectives. In *Linguistics, Archaeology and the Human Past*, ed. T. Osada and H. Endo, pp. 125–188. Kyoto: Research Institute for Humanity and Nature.

Parzinger, H. 2007. *Im Zeichen des goldenen Greifen: Königsgräber der Skythen.* Munich: Prestel.

Perrot, J., and D. Ladiray. 1988. *Les hommes de Mallaha (Eynan) Israel.* Memoires et Travaux du Centre de Recherche Français de Jerusalem 7. Paris: Association Paleorient.

Petersen, R. 1964. The Greenland Tupilak. *Folk* 6 (2): 71–101.

Petrie, W.M.F. 1914. *Amulets.* London: Constable.

———. 1921. *Corpus of Prehistoric Pottery and Palettes.* London: British School of Archaeology in Egypt.

Petrie, W.M.F., G. A. Wainwright, and A. H. Gardiner. 1913. *Tarkhan I and Memphis V.* London: School of Archaeology in Egypt.

Pettinato, G. 1991. *Ebla: A New Look at History*, trans. C. Faith Richardson. Baltimore: Johns Hopkins University Press.

Philip, G. 2002. Contacts between the "Uruk" world and the Levant during the fourth millennium BC: evidence and interpretation. In *Artefacts of Complexity*, ed. J. N. Postgate, pp. 207–235. Warminster, UK: Aris and Phillips.

Phillips, J. 2008. *Aegyptiaca on the Island of Crete in Their Chronological Context: A Critical Review*. 2 volumes. Vienna: Österreichiscen Akademie der Wissenschaften.

Pinker, S. 1994. *The Language Instinct: The New Science of Language and Mind*. London: Allen Lane.

Pittman, H. 1994. Towards an understanding of the role of glyptic imagery in the administrative systems of proto-literate Greater Mesopotamia. In *Archives before Writing*, ed. P. Ferioli, E. Fiandra, G. G. Fissore, and M. Frangipane, pp. 177–204. Rome: Ministero per i beni culturali e ambientali, Ufficio centrale per i beni archivistici.

———. 1995. Cylinder seals and scarabs in the ancient Near East. In *Civilizations of the Ancient Near East*, ed. J. M. Sasson, pp. 1589–1603. New York: Scribner.

———. 1996. Constructing context: the Gebel el-Arak knife. Greater Mesopotamian and Egyptian interaction in the late fourth millennium BC. In *The Study of the Ancient Near East in the Twenty-first Century: The William Foxwell Albright Centennial Conference*, ed. J. S. Cooper and G. M. Schwartz, pp. 9–32. Winona Lake, IN: Eisenbrauns.

———. 1997. The administrative function of glyptic art in Proto-Elamite Iran: a survey of the evidence. In *Sceaux d'Orient et leur emploi*, ed. R. Gyselen, pp. 133–162. Res Orientalis 10. Leuven: Peeters.

———. 2001. Mesopotamian intraregional relations reflected through glyptic evidence in the Late Chalcolithic 1–5 periods. In *Uruk Mesopotamia and Its Neighbors: Cross-Cultural Interactions in the Era of State Formation*, ed. M. S. Rothman, pp. 403–444. Santa Fe: School of American Research.

———. 2002. The "Jeweler's" seal from Susa and art of Awan. In *Leaving No Stones Unturned: Essays on the Ancient Near East and Egypt in Honor of Donald P. Hansen*, ed. E. Ehrenberg, pp. 211–236. Winona Lake, IN: Eisenbrauns.

Pollock, S. 1999. *Ancient Mesopotamia: The Eden That Never Was*. Cambridge, UK: Cambridge University Press.

Porada, E. 1985. Syrian seals from the late fourth to the late second millennium. In *Ebla to Damascus: Art and Archaeology of Ancient Syria: An Exhibition from the Directorate-General of Antiquities and Museums, Syrian Arab Republic*, ed. H. Weiss, pp. 90–104. Washington, DC: Smithsonian Institution Traveling Exhibition Service.

———. 1995. *Man and Images in the Ancient Near East* (with "Discussion" by F.A.M. Wiggermann). Wakefield, RI, and London: Moyer Bell.

Possehl, G. L. 2002. *The Indus Civilization: A Contemporary Perspective*. Walnut Creek, CA, and Oxford, UK: AltaMira.

Potts, D. T. 1990. *The Arabian Gulf in Antiquity*. Volume 1. *From Prehistory to the Fall of the Achaemenid Empire*. Oxford, UK: Clarendon Press.

———. 1997. *Mesopotamian Civilization: The Material Foundations*. London: Athlone.

———. 1999. *The Archaeology of Elam: Formation and Transformation of an Ancient Iranian State*. Cambridge, UK: Cambridge University Press.

Potts, T. F. 1994. *Mesopotamia and the East: An Archaeological and Historical Study of Foreign Relations ca. 3400–2000 B.C.* Oxford, UK: Oxford University Committee for Archaeology.

Poulsen, F. 1912. *Der Orient und die frühgriechische Kunst*. Leibzig: B. G. Teubner.

Powell, A., S. Shennan, and M. G. Thomas. 2009. Late Pleistocene demography and the appearance of modern human behavior. *Science* 324: 1298–1301.

Puett, M. J. 2002. *To Become a God: Cosmology, Sacrifice, and Self-divinization in Early China*. Cambridge, MA: Harvard-Yenching Institute.

Pyysiäinen, I. 2001. *How Religion Works: Towards a New Cognitive Science of Religion*. Leiden: Brill.

Quack, J. F. 2009. The animals of the desert and the return of the goddess. In *Desert Animals in the Eastern Sahara: Status, Economic Significance, and Cultural Reflection in Antiquity*, Colloquium Africanum 4, ed. H. Reimer, F. Förster, M. Herb, and N. Pöllath, pp. 341–361. Cologne: Heinrich-Barth-Institute.

Quibell, J. E. 1898. Slate palette from Hieraconpolis. *Zeitschrift für Ägyptische Sprache und Altertumskunde* 36: 81–86.

Radner, K. 2005. Kubaba und die Fische: Bemerkungen zur Herrin von Karkemiš. In *Von Sumer bis Homer: Festschrift für Manfred Schretter zum 60. Geburtstag am 25. Februar 2004*, ed. R. Rollinger, pp. 543–556. Münster: Ugarit-Verlag.

———. 2009. The Assyrian king and his scholars: the Syro-Anatolian and the Egyptian schools. In *Of God(s), Trees, Kings, and Scholars: Neo-Assyrian and Related Studies in Honour of Simo Parpola*, ed. M. Luukko, S. Svärd, and R. Mattila, pp. 221–238. Helsinki: Finnish Oriental Society.

Rasmussen, K. 1921. *Eskimo Folk-Tales*, trans. W. Worster. London: Gyldendal.

Rawson, J. 1987. *Chinese Bronzes: Art and Ritual*. London: British Museum.

Reinhold, M. 1946. Historian of the classical world: a critique of Rostovtzeff. *Science and Society* 10 (4): 361–391.

Reisner, G. A. 1923. *Excavations at Kerma*. Cambridge, MA: Peabody Museum of Harvard University.

Renfrew, C., C. Frith, and L. Malfouris. 2009. *The Sapient Mind: Archaeology Meets Neuroscience*. Oxford, UK: Oxford University Press.

Renfrew, C., and C. Scarre. 1998. *Cognition and Material Culture: The Archaeology of Symbolic Storage*. Cambridge, UK: McDonald Institute.

Richerson, P. J., and R. Boyd. 2005. *Not by Genes Alone: How Culture Transformed Human Evolution*. Chicago and London: University of Chicago Press.

Richter, I. 2008 [1952]. *Leonardo da Vinci: The Notebooks* (with a preface by M. Kemp and introduction by T. Wells). Oxford, UK: Oxford University Press.

Riegl, A. 1893. *Stilfragen: Grundlegungen zu einer Geschichte der Ornamentik*. Berlin: Georg Siemens.

———. 1992 [1893]. *Problems of Style: Foundations for a History of Ornament*, trans. E. Kain, ed. D. Castriota. Princeton, NJ: Princeton University Press.

———. 2000 [1900]. The place of the Vapheio cups in the history of art. In *The Vienna School Reader: Politics and Art Historical Method in the 1930s*, ed. C. S. Wood, pp. 105–127. New York: Zone.

Rittig, D. 1977. *Assyrisch-babylonische Kleinplastik magischer Bedeutung vom 13.–6. Jh. v. Chr.* Munich: Verlag Uni-Druck.

Riva, C., and N. Vella, eds. 2006. *Debating Orientalization: Multidisciplinary Approaches to Change in the Ancient Mediterranean*. London: Equinox.

Roach, K. J. 2009. *The Elamite Cylinder Seal Corpus, c. 3500–1000 BC*. Unpublished doctoral dissertation, University of Sydney.

Robins, G. 1994. *Proportion and Style in Ancient Egyptian Art*. London: Thames and Hudson.

Romm, J. 1992. *The Edges of the Earth in Ancient Thought: Geography, Exploration, and Fiction*. Princeton, NJ: Princeton University Press.

Rostovtzeff, M. I. 1920. The Sumerian treasure of Astrabad. *Journal of Egyptian Archaeology* 6 (1): 4–27.

———. 1922. *Iranians and Greeks in South Russia*. Oxford, UK: Clarendon Press.

———. 1926a. *A History of the Ancient World, Volume 1: The Orient and Greece*, trans. J. D. Duff. Oxford, UK: Clarendon Press.

———. 1926b. *The Social and Economic History of the Roman Empire*. Oxford, UK: Clarendon Press.

———. 1929. *The Animal Style in South Russia and China, being the Material of a Course of Lectures delivered in August 1925 at Princeton University under the auspices of the Harvard-Princeton Fine Arts Club*. Princeton Monographs in Art and Archaeology 14. Princeton, NJ: Princeton University Press; London: H. Milford, Oxford University Press.

Rostovtzeff, M. I. 1932. *Caravan Cities*, trans. D. and T. Talbot Rice. Oxford, UK: Clarendon Press.

———. 1941. *The Social and Economic History of the Hellenistic World*. 3 volumes. Oxford, UK: Clarendon Press.

Rova, E. 2008. Response to D. Wengrow (2008). *Current Anthropology* 49: 24–25.

Rova, E., and H. Weiss, eds. 2003. *The Origins of North Mesopotamian Civilization: Ninevite 5 Chronology, Economy, Society*. Turnhout: Brepols.

Rudenko, S. I. 1970. *Frozen Tombs of Siberia: The Pazyryk Burials of Iron Age Horsemen*, trans. M. W. Thompson. London: Dent.

Runciman, W. G. 1982. Origins of states: the case of Archaic Greece. *Journal of Comparative Study of Society and History* 24: 351–377.

Russell, N., and K. J. McGowan. 2003. Dance of the cranes: crane symbolism at Çatalhöyük and beyond. *Antiquity* 77: 445–455.

Sadek, A. I. 1987. *Popular Religion in Egypt during the New Kingdom*. Hildesheim: Gerstenberg.

Salje, B. 1990. *Der "Common Style" der Mitanni-Glyptik und die Glyptik der Levante und Zyperns in der späten Bronzezeit*. Mainz am Rhein: Phillip von Zabern.

Sarianidi, V. I. 1981. Seal-amulets of the Murghab style. In *The Bronze Age Civilization of Central Asia*, ed. P. Kohl, pp. 221–255. New York: Sharpe.

Sax, M., and N. D. Meeks. 1994. The introduction of wheel cutting as a technique for engraving cylinder seals: its distinction from filing. *Iraq* 56: 153–166.

Schäfer, H. 1986 [1919]. *Principles of Egyptian Art*, trans. and ed. John Baines. Oxford, UK: Griffith Institute.

Schapiro, M. 2000 [1936]. The New Viennese School. In *The Vienna School Reader: Politics and Art Historical Method in the 1930s*, ed. C. S. Wood, pp. 453–485. New York: Zone.

Schlager, N. 1996. Phangromouro I and II: two recently discovered paleontological sites, with a note on Hogarth's Zakros sealings nos. 92 and 139. In *Pleistocene and Holocene Fauna of Crete and Its First Settlers*, ed. D. S. Reese, pp. 33–45. Madison: Prehistory Press.

Schmandt-Besserat, D. 1993. Images of Enship. In *Between the Rivers and over the Mountains: Archaeologica Anatolica et Mesopotamica Alba Palmieri Dedicata*, ed. M. Frangipane, H. Hauptmann, M. Liverani, P. Matthiae, and M. Mellink, pp. 201–220. Rome: Università di Roma "La Sapienza."

Schmid, E. (with contributions by J. Hahn and U. Wolf). 1989. Die altsteinzeitliche Elfenbeinstatuette aus der Höhle Stadel im Hohlenstein bei Asselfingen, Alb-Donau-Kreis. *Fundberichte aus Baden-Württemberg* 14: 33–118.

Schmidt, K. 2006. *Sie bauten die ersten Tempel: das rätselhafte Heiligtum der Steinzeitjäger; die archäologische Entdeckung am Göbekli Tepe*. Munich: Beck.

Schoep, I. 2006. Looking beyond the first palaces: elites and the agency of power in EMIII-MMII Crete. *American Journal of Archaeology* 110: 37–64.

Scholl, B. J., and A. M. Leslie. 1999. Modularity, development and "theory of mind." *Mind and Language* 14: 131–153.

Scott, F. J., and S. Baron-Cohen. 1996. Imagining real and unreal things: evidence of a dissociation in autism. *Journal of Cognitive Neuroscience* 8 (4): 371–382.

Scott, J. C. 1998. *Seeing Like a State: How Certain Schemes to Improve the Human Condition Have Failed*. New Haven, CT, and London: Yale University Press.

Scurlock, J. A. 2006. *Magico-medical Means of Treating Ghost-induced Illnesses in Ancient Mesopotamia*. Leiden: Brill/Styx.

Shennan, S. 2002. *Genes, Memes and Human History*. London: Thames and Hudson.

Sher, Y. A. 1988. On the sources of Scythic animal style. *Arctic Anthropology* 25 (2): 47–60.

Sherratt, A. G., and E. S. Sherratt. 1991. From luxuries to commodities: the nature of Mediterranean Bronze Age trading systems. In *Bronze Age Trade in the Mediterranean*, ed. N. Gale, pp. 351–386. Jonsered: Paul Åström.

———. 1998. Small worlds: interaction and identity in the ancient Mediterranean. In *The Aegean and the Orient in the Second Millennium. Proceedings of the 50th Anniversary Symposium Cincinnati, 18–20 April 1997*, ed. E. H. Cline and D. Harris-Cline, pp. 329–343. Liège: Histoire de l'art et archéologie de la Grèce antique; Austin: University of Texas at Austin.

Sherratt, E. S. 1994. Comment on Ora Negbi, The "Libyan landscape" from Thera: a review of Aegean enterprises overseas in the Late Minoan IA Period. *Journal of Mediterranean Archaeology* 7: 237–240.

Smith, W. S. 1965. *Interconnections in the Ancient Near East*. New Haven, CT: Yale University Press.

Smits, M. 2006. Taming monsters: the cultural domestication of new technology. *Technology in Society* 28: 489–504.

Solecki, R. L. 1977. Predatory bird rituals at Zawi Chemi Shanidar. *Sumer* 33: 42–47.

Solomon, A. 1997. The myth of ritual origins: ethnography, mythology and interpretation of San rock art. *South African Archaeological Bulletin* 52 (165): 3–13.

Sonik, K. 2010. *Daimon-haunted Universe: Conceptions of the Supernatural in Mesopotamia*. Unpublished doctoral dissertation, University of Pennsylvania.

Sperber, D. 1975. Pourquoi les animaux parfaits, les hybrides et les monstres sont-ils bons à penser symboliquement? *L'Homme* 15 (2): 5–34.

———. 1985. Anthropology and psychology: towards an epidemiology of representations. *Man* 20 (1): 73–89.

———. 1996a. *Explaining Culture: A Naturalistic Approach*. Oxford, UK: Blackwell.

———. 1996b. Why are perfect animals, hybrids, and monsters food for symbolic thought? *Method and Theory in the Study of Religion* 8: 143–169.

Sperber, D., and L. A. Hirschfeld. 2004. The cognitive foundations of cultural stability and diversity. *Trends in Cognitive Sciences* 8: 40–46.

Stafford, B. M. 2007. *Echo Objects: The Cognitive Work of Images*. Chicago and London: University of Chicago Press.

Stevens, A. 2009. Domestic religions practices. In *UCLA Encyclopedia of Egyptology*, ed. W. Wendrich and J. Dieleman. Los Angeles. Available at http://escholarship.org/uc/item/7s07628w (accessed 08/15/2012).

Strickland, D. H. 2003. *Saracens, Demons, and Jews: Making Monsters in Medieval Art*. Princeton, NJ, and Oxford, UK: Princeton University Press.

Szpakowska, K. 2009. Demons in ancient Egypt. *Religious Compass* 3: 799–805.

Taborin, Y., M. Christensen, M. Olive, N. Pigeot, C. Fritz, and G. Tosello. 2001. De l'art magdalénien figuratif à Etiolles (Essonne, Bassin parisien). *Bulletin de la Société Préhistorique Française* 98: 125–132.

Teissier, B. 1987. Glyptic evidence for a connection between Iran, Syro-Palestine and Egypt in the fourth and third millennia. *Iran* 25: 27–53.

Tomasello, M. 1999. *The Cultural Origins of Human Cognition*. Cambridge, MA: Harvard University Press.

Török, László. 2009. *Between Two Worlds: The Frontier Region between Ancient Nubia and Egypt, 3700 BC–500 AD*. Leiden: Brill.

Tourtet, F. 2010. Demons at home: the presence of demonic figures in the ancient Near Eastern domestic architecture. In *Dūr-Katlimmu 2008 and Beyond*, ed. H. Kühne, pp. 241–265. Wiesbaden: Harrassowitz.

Trigger, B. G. 1989. *A History of Archaeological Thought*. Cambridge, UK: Cambridge University Press.

Turner, V. W. 1969. *The Ritual Process: Structure and Anti-Structure*. London: Routledge and Kegan Paul.

Ucko, P., and A. Rosenfeld. 1967. *Palaeolithic Cave Art*. London: Weidenfeld and Nicolson.

van Buren, E. D. 1931. *Foundation Figurines and Offerings*. Berlin: H. Schoetz & Co.

Vandermeersch, B. 1970. Une sepulture moustérienne avec offrandes découverte dans la grotte de Qafzeh. *Comptes Rendus Hebdomadaires des Séances de l'Académie des Sciences* 270: 298–301.

van Lepp, J. 1999. The misidentification of the predynastic Egyptian bull's head amulet. *Göttinger Miszellen* 168: 101–111.

van Neer, W., V. Linseele, and R. F. Friedman. 2004. Animal burials and food offerings at the elite cemetery HK6 of Hierakonpolis. In *Egypt at Its Origins: Studies in Memory of Barbara Adams*, ed. S. Hendrickx, R. F. Friedman, K. M. Ciałowicz, and M. Chłodnicki, pp. 67–130. Leuven: Peeters.

Verbrugghe, G. P., and Wickersham, J. M. 2001. *Berossos and Manetho, Introduced and Translated: Native Traditions in Ancient Mesopotamia and Egypt*. Ann Arbor: University of Michigan Press.

Vernant, J.-P. 1991. Death in the eyes: Gorgo, figure of the Other. In *Mortals and Immortals: Collected Essays*, ed. F. I. Zeitlin, pp. 111–140. Princeton, NJ: Princeton University Press.

Wang Haicheng. Forthcoming. China's first empire? Interpreting the material record of the Erligang expansion. In *Art and Archaeology of the Erligang Civilization*, ed. K. Steinke. Princeton, NJ: Princeton University Press for Tang Center.

Ward, C. A. 2003. Sewn plank boats from Early Dynastic Abydos, Egypt. In *Boats, Ships and Shipyards: Proceedings of the Ninth International Symposium on Boat and Ship Archaeology, Venice 2000*, ed. C. Beltrame, pp. 19–23. Oxford, UK: Oxbow.

Ward, W. A. 1978. *Studies on Scarab Seals, Volume 1. Pre-12th Dynasty Scarab Amulets*. Warminster, UK: Aris and Phillips.

Warren, P. M. 1995. Minoan Crete and Pharaonic Egypt. In *Egypt, the Aegean, and the Levant: Interconnections in the Second Millennium BC*, ed. W. V. Davies and L. Schofield, pp. 1–18. London: British Museum Press.

Watkins, T. 2002. Memes, memeplexes and the emergence of religion in the Neolithic. In *Magical Practices and Ritual in the Near East Neolithic*, Studies in Early Near Eastern Production, Subsistence, and Environment 9, ed. H. G. Gebel, B. D. Hermansen, and C. H. Jensen, pp. 41–48. Berlin: Ex Oriente.

Watrous, L. V. 2004. *The Plain of Phaistos: Cycles of Social Complexity in the Mesara Region of Crete*. Los Angeles: Cotsen Institute of Archaeology at UCLA.

Webb, J. M. 1999. *Ritual Architecture, Iconography and Practice in the Late Cypriot Bronze Age*. Jonsered: Åström.

Weeks, K. R. 1971. *The Anatomical Knowledge of the Ancient Egyptians and the Representation of the Human Figure in Egyptian Art*. Ann Arbor: University Microfilms International.

Weingarten, J. 1983. *The Zakro Master and His Place in Prehistory*. Göteborg: Paul Åströms Förlag.

———. 1986. The sealing structures of Minoan Crete: MM II Phaistos to the destruction of the palace of Knossos. Part 1: The evidence until the LM IB destructions. *Oxford Journal of Archaeology* 5: 279–298.

———. 1991. *The Transformation of Egyptian Taweret into the Minoan Genius: A Study in Cultural Transmission in the Middle Bronze Age*. Studies in Mediterranean Archaeology 88. Partille: P. Åströms.

———. 2010. Some Minoan Minoan-Genii on LC III Cyprus. In *Researches in Cypriote History and Archaeology*, ed. A. M. Jasink and L. Bombardieri, pp. 95–102. Florence: Firenze University Press.

Wengrow, D. 1998. The changing face of clay: continuity and change in the transition from village to urban life in the Near East. *Antiquity* 72: 783–795.

———. 2001a. *Comparative Animal Art of the Neolithic Fertile Crescent and Nile Valley: A Long-Term Perspective on State Formation*. Unpublished doctoral dissertation, University of Oxford.

———. 2001b. The evolution of simplicity: aesthetic labour and social change in the Neolithic Near East. *World Archaeology* 33: 168–188.

———. 2003. Interpreting animal art in the prehistoric Near East. In *Culture through Objects: Ancient Near Eastern Studies in Honour of P.R.S. Moorey*, ed. T. F. Potts, M. Roaf, and D. Stein, pp. 139–160. Oxford, UK: Griffith Institute.

———. 2006. *The Archaeology of Early Egypt: Social Transformations in North-East Africa, 10,000 to 2650 BC*. Cambridge, UK: Cambridge University Press.

———. 2008. Prehistories of commodity branding. *Current Anthropology* 49: 7–34.

———. 2010a. The voyages of Europa: ritual and trade in the Eastern Mediterranean circa 2300–1850 BC. In W. A. Parkinson and M. L. Galaty, eds. (2010), pp. 141–160.

———. 2010b. *What Makes Civilization? The Ancient Near East and the Future of the West*. Oxford, UK: Oxford University Press.

Wengrow, D., and J. Baines. 2004. Images, human bodies, and the ritual construction of memory in late predynastic Egypt. In *Egypt at Its Origins: Studies in Memory of Barbara Adams*, ed. S. Hendrickx, R. F. Friedman, K. M. Ciałowicz, and M. Chłodnicki, pp. 1081–1114. Leuven: Peeters.

Wes, M. A. 1990. *Michael Rostovtzeff, Historian in Exile: Russian Roots in an American Context.* Stuttgart: Franz Steiner.

White, R. 1992. Beyond art: toward an understanding of the origins of material representation in Europe. *Annual Review of Anthropology* 21: 537–564.

———. 2003. *Prehistoric Art: The Symbolic Journey of Humankind.* New York: Harry N. Abrams.

Whitehouse, Harvey. 2004. *Modes of Religiosity: A Cognitive Theory of Religion.* Walnut Creek, CA: AltaMira.

Whitehouse, Helen. 2002. A decorated knife handle from the "main deposit" at Hierakonpolis. *Mitteilungen des Deutschen Archäologischen Instituts, Abteilung Kairo* 58: 425–446.

Whitley, J. 1988. Early states and hero cults: a reappraisal. *Journal of Hellenic Studies* 108: 173–182.

———. 1994. Protoattic pottery: a contextual approach. In *Classical Greece: Ancient Histories and Modern Archaeologies*, ed. I. Morris, pp.51–70. Cambridge, UK: Cambridge University Press.

Wickede, A. von. 1990. *Prähistorische Stempelglyptik in Vorderasien.* Munich: Profil Verlag.

Wiggermann, F.A.M. 1992. *Mesopotamian Protective Spirits: The Ritual Texts.* Groningen: Styx and PP Publications.

———. 1994. Mischwesen. A. In *Reallexikon der Assyriologie und Vorderasiatischen Archäologie* 8, ed. E. Ebeling and B. Meissner, pp. 222–246. Berlin: de Gruyter.

———. 1996. Scenes from the shadow side. In *Mesopotamian Poetic Language: Sumerian and Akkadian*, ed. M. E. Vogelzang and H.L.J. Vanstiphout, pp. 207–230. Groningen: Styx.

Wilcke, C. 1972–1975. Huwawa/Humbaba. In *Reallexikon der Assyriologie* 4, ed. D. O. Edzard, pp. 530–535. Berlin and New York: De Gruyter.

Winkler-Horaček, L. 2008. Fiktionale Grenzräume im frühen Griechenland. In *Mensch und Tier in der Antike. Grenzziehung und Grenzüberschreitung*, ed. A. Alexandridis, M. Wild, and L. Winkler-Horaček, pp. 503–525. Wiesbaden: Reichert.

———. 2011. *Monster in der frühgriechischen Kunst.* Berlin: De Gruyter.

Winter, I. 1995. Homer's Phoenicians: history, ethnography, or literary trope? A perspective on early Orientalism. In *The Ages of Homer: A Tribute to Emily Townsend Vermeule*, ed. J. B. Carter and S. P. Morris, pp. 247–272. Austin: University of Texas Press.

Winter, N. A. 1993. *Greek Architectural Terracottas from the Prehistoric to the End of the Archaic Period.* Oxford, UK: Clarendon Press.

Wittkower, R. 1942. Marvels of the East: a study in the history of monsters. *Journal of the Warburg and Courtauld Institutes* 5: 159–197.

Yablonsky, L. T. 2010. New excavations of the early nomadic burial ground at Filippovka (Southern Ural Region, Russia). *American Journal of Archaeology* 114: 129–143.

Yoffee, N. 2005. *Myths of the Archaic State: Evolution of the Earliest Cities, States, and Civilizations.* Cambridge, UK: Cambridge University Press.

Yoffee, N., and J. J. Clark, eds. 1993. *Early Stages in the Evolution of Mesopotamian Civilization: Soviet Excavations in Northern Iraq.* Tucson: University of Arizona Press.

Zarins, J. 1978. Steatite vessels in the Riyadh Museum. *Atlal* 2: 65–94.

Zhongpei, Z. 2005. The Yangshao period: prosperity and the transformation of prehistoric society. In *The Formation of Chinese Civilization: An Archaeological Perspective*, ed. S. Allen, pp. 43–84. New Haven, CT, and London: Yale University Press.

Zuckerman, S. 2008. Fit for a (not-quite-so-great) king: a faience lion-headed cup from Hazor. *Levant* 40 (1): 115–125.

INDEX

Abydos (Egypt), 45–47
Afghanistan, 60
Arabia, 60, 64, 96–98
Arnheim, Rudolph, 24–25, 28, 75
art: "animal style," 9, 18; "international style," 94–95; Neolithic, 37–43, 51; "orientalizing," 12–15, 17, 28, 91–92, 115n14; Paleolithic, 33–37, 51, 118n14, 118n15; predynastic (Egyptian), 43–49, 121n47
Assur (Iraq), 99
Ataç, Mehmet-Ali, 105
autism, 118n15

Bactria-Margiana culture (Turkmenistan), 61, 64
Bagley, Robert, 85
Baxandall, Michael, 113n12
Benjamin, Walter, 1
Bevan, Andrew, 90
Breuil, Henri, 34–36
bronze vessels, 83–87
Bowersock, Glenn, 8
Boyer, Pascal, 22–23, 80
bureaucracy, 70–73, 89; "bureaucratic eye", 71

Canetti, Elias, 117n35
canon, 2, 90
Çatalhöyük (Turkey), 42–43, 120n30
Caucasus, 11, 100
Cauvin, Jacques, 39
ceramics, 43, 45–47
Childe, V. Gordon, 12
China, 7, 9, 18, 83–87
classification, 5–6, 21–22
cognition, 3–7, 19–24, 82, 110–112
composite figuration, 24–28, 69–73
counterintuitive representations, 22–24, 50, 80, 102, 110
Crete, 61, 63–64, 75, 92
cuneiform script, 69–71
cyclops, 79

cylinder seals. *See* seals
Cyprus, 79

demons, 26, 56, 100–104
Descola, Philippe, 26, 116n25
diffusionism, 16
diplomacy, 95, 108
dragon, 5, 17

Ebla (Syria), 61
Egypt, 105–106, 131n41; Neolithic, 43–45; predynastic, 43–49; protodynastic, 51–59, 62, 92–94
Elsner, Jas, 12
"epidemiology of culture." *See* cognition; evolutionary psychology
evolutionary psychology, 3, 20, 50, 88–89, 111, 115n4. *See also* cognition

farming (origins of), 39
Feldman, Marian, 95
Frankfort, Henri, 1, 12

Göbekli Tepe (Turkey), 40
gods, 25, 39, 121n16
Gombrich, Ernst, 82, 85
gorgoneion, 77–78, 103
Göttertypentext, 75
Greece: Bronze Age, 12–13, 61, 63–64, 78–79, 92; Iron Age, 9, 13, 17–18, 80, 90–91
griffin, 5, 17, 62–64, 124n42, 124n43, 129n12

Hallowell, A. Irving, 4
Hierakonpolis (Egypt), 45
Houma (China), 86
Humbaba, 77, 80
hunter-gatherers, 30–32, 34–40, 44, 110; Inuit, 30–31, 117n32; San, 31, 36

immunology, 107
Indus Valley, 60, 64, 98